נשמת ירושלים

The Soul of Yerushalayim

Personalities, Places, and Moments
in the Courtyards of Yerushalayim
and Its Neighborhoods

PHOTOGRAPHY: BARUCH YAARI   •   TEXT: ARYEH EHRLICH

FELDHEIM PUBLISHERS
JERUSALEM   NEW YORK

Photography: Baruch Yaari
Text: Aryeh Ehrlich
Translation: Dina Harris
Editing: Chava Grossman / Rabbi David Kahn
Proofreading: Tziporah Frankel
Hebrew edition design: Esther Bezalel Studio
Design adapted for this edition: Michael Silverstein

Hebrew Edition published as *Nishmas Yerushalayim*, 2019

ISBN 978-1-68025-516-4

Copyright © 2021 by Baruch Yaari
www.b-yaary.co.il | byaary@gmail.com

All rights reserved.
No part of this publication may be translated, reproduced, stored in a retrieval system or transmitted, in any form or by any means, electronic, mechanical, photocopying, recording or otherwise, even for personal use, without written permission from the publisher.

FELDHEIM PUBLISHERS
POB 43163 / Jerusalem, Israel

208 Airport Executive Park
Nanuet, NY 10954
www.feldheim.com

Distributed in Europe by:
LEHMANNS
+44-0-191-430-0333
info@lehmanns.co.uk
www.lehmanns.co.uk

Distributed in Australia by:
GOLDS WORLD OF JUDAICA
+613 95278775
info@golds.com.au
www.golds.com.au

Printed in Israel

Contents

Introduction The City of the Soul / Aryeh Ehrlich 4
  Snapshots of My Life / Baruch Yaari 10

Chapter 1: Shabbos 17
Chapter 2: Anshei Yerushalayim 63
Chapter 3: Batei Midrashos 101
Chapter 4: The Children of Yerushalayim 137
Chapter 5: The Month of Nissan 185
Chapter 6: Lag Ba'Omer 221
Chapter 7: The Month of Sivan 239
Chapter 8: Exile and Consolation 259
Chapter 9: The Days of Awe 271
Chapter 10: Sukkos 297
Chapter 11: Chanukah 339
Chapter 12: Tu Bi'Shevat 355
Chapter 13: Purim 365

Afterword 396

בעיר הנשמה / אריה ארליך
The City of the Soul / Aryeh Ehrlich

A Rainy, Wintery Friday Night in Yerushalayim, 1990

A small boy with curly *peyos* stands before an Aron Kodesh. Supported by two giant pillars, adorned with carvings of grape leaves, grapes, and flowers, the ornate Aron Kodesh graces the front wall of the ancient shul in Meah Shearim. The image is disproportionate: a tiny figure on the steps of a huge monument. The Aron Kodesh is two stories high and more than one hundred years old — the same age as the shul that was built in 1889. The boy is just three feet tall, and only three and a half years old.

Behind him stand the elderly Chassidim of Meah Shearim, Torah greats and Chassidish giants, accepting Shabbos with a Lecha Dodi that ascends with lofty Chassidish devotion. There is a mix of voices; some hoarse, some clear, some loud, and some soft.

Soaked with ancient *tefillos*, the fragrance of old-time Yerushalayim emanates from the thick walls. The furniture is archaic; the Aron Kodesh is ancient, built in the style prevalent at that time. The scent of generations gone by is preserved; the walls are permeated with echoes of the past, decades of *avodas Hashem* in the Chassidish *nusach* of yesteryear.

In front of the *amud*, next to the Aron Kodesh, stands an elderly chazzan with a flowing white beard. His back is hunched and his moustache is stained yellow from years of sniffing snuff. He's singing *"Kol Hashem yecholel ayalos vayechesof ye'aros u'vheichalo kulo omer kavod."*

The little boy stands to his left. Underneath the tall pillar on the right side of the Aron Kodesh, he opens a small cupboard and fumbles around. Inside is a silver box with *besamim* cloves, blackened over the years. There is a silver holder for the Havdalah candle, an old, braided wax candle, matches, remnants of the sweet red wine used for Kiddush and Havdalah, and a tin cup which the elder Yerushalmis refer to as *"De Schiff"* — the ship — because of its unique shape. This cup was passed from hand to hand during Shalosh Seudos to wash for *mayim acharonim*.

The boy does the same thing every Shabbos: he goes to the small *muktzeh* cupboard, plays with the candles and sniffs the familiar fragrance of the *besamim*, unaware of its significance, happily occupied until the end of davening.

One Shabbos, his game was interrupted.

He was groping for something in the cupboard, completely oblivious to the davening taking place behind him, trying with all his childish might to attach the beeswax candle to its ancient base. Suddenly, he felt a pair of shaky hands grasp hold of him and lift him high. Surprised by this unexpected ride, he landed on a bench nearby.

The person carrying him was awe-inspiring; a man the boy related to with *yiras romemus,* Rav Moshe Weber *zt"l*. The Rav, a leader of *Yerushalayim shel Maalah*, had decided it was time to educate the child, a boy old enough to understand that you don't touch *muktzeh* on Shabbos — and certainly not at the front of the shul. Rav Moshe handed a *pekele* to the confused child with a caress — compensation for his embarrassment. Needless to say, the boy never went to the *muktzeh* cabinet again.

I was that little boy.

Childhood in Batei Ungarin was a life of innocence and simplicity. It was a pure childhood that absorbed little from the poisonous, contaminated world outside.

When I think of that refined, faultless, pure innocence, a great yearning grabs hold of me, grasps onto my *neshamah* and surrounds me. Perhaps there were other flaws — no place is perfect — but the advantages are irrefutable. Generous, heaping measures of straightforward innocence guided its people, especially the children, whose world consisted only of what happened within their fiercely guarded *dalet amos*.

Although I know that some may perceive my words as an embellished perception or an attempt to glorify the place where I grew up (after all, people tend to paint their childhood with nostalgic colors), I write them nonetheless.

But this isn't the purpose. Over the years, I have critiqued some of the things that happened between the curved alleys and closed walls of the ancient neighborhood. Although I haven't yet grown old, only a hint of the spirit of Batei Ungarin remains inside me. My visits to the old neighborhood are a mixture of sweet nostalgia and a bit of dissonance when I sense the new spirit that has taken hold there. I remember the glorious personalities who adorned the neighborhood's shuls, and against the backdrop of its lofty past, the present seems a little faded.

Still, this neighborhood, one of the neighborhoods of the Yishuv Hayashan, has plenty of sweetness and goodness, illumination and purity.

Try as I might to turn the wheel of my life, the hand of *hashgachah* takes control. There are no coincidences. If I was born in Batei Ungarin, then a piece of that neighborhood, of the Yishuv Hayashan, is embedded in my soul. I could have been born in another city or perhaps in one of the more modern Yerushalayim neighborhoods and would have had to learn about the Yishuv Hayashan from another author, but The One in Charge wanted me to be that author, to write about the Yerushalayim of old for those who grew up elsewhere.

Our Sages taught us that every city and country has a heavenly minister in charge of its affairs. Accordingly, I believe that every city has its own *neshamah*. Just as each person has a physical body that houses a holy *neshamah* and spiritual form, every city, with its stones and streets and pathways and bridges, has a *neshamah* as well.

Yerushalayim has a different *neshamah* — a *neshamah shel Maalah*. The *neshamah* of Yerushalayim is hewed from the halo of the *Shechinah*. It reaches the heavens and breathes the air of Gan Eden. *Yerushalayim shel Mattah* is nourished by *Yerushalayim shel Maalah*, its heavenly counterpart. We see this as well in the form and spirit of its people. *Chen ha'ir al yoshveha*. The residents of the Yishuv Hayashan preserved the ancient Yerushalmi flavor and exuded their charm on the city itself.

Yerushalayim is old in days, but young in spirit, since its spirit is renewed every single day. There is no present moment in Yerushalayim. The shadows of the past overpower the present, like the proverbial *"kankan chadash malei yashan"* — the new pitcher filled with old wine.

Yerushalayim is a city of alleyways, walls, and shadows, but more than anything, it is a city of people: a city of Jews who serve their Creator with simplicity and sincerity, where the clothing has the same "zebra stripes" and wide-brimmed hats (the "super") as the Yishuv Hayashan, where the names stay the same from generation to generation. Their dress and demeanor recalls a time when the distinguished residents wore their finery to greet the *mara d'asra*, Rav Yosef Chaim Sonnenfeld *zt"l*.

Again I find myself trapped in externalities. Instead of describing clothes, I should discuss the internal dimension, the Yerushalami spirit that rests behind this distinct way of dress. It's an ancient, pure, beautiful spirit that hasn't been blemished by the passing years, hasn't submitted to modernization, and hasn't been influenced by the passage of time. Those with sharp vision and understanding can see the complete, inner-focused, strong Yerushalmi character that hides beneath the white, pom-pom-topped yarmulke.

The Yerushalayim of my childhood was a city of clotheslines stretched above wooden beams; of righteous women paddling old, worn mattresses on Erev Pesach; of Jews going out at midnight to serve their Creator. It is a city of big *shtreimels* — elegant, though worn — that are taken out every Erev Shabbos, when Jews with wet *peyos* stride in the gold-striped tunics that are covered by the thin brown coat known as the *djubeh*.

My Yerushalayim is a city of Torah personalities, *talmidei chachamim* and *geonim*, who blend into the curves in the paths, walking humbly and silently on the side of the road, demanding no attention. This is a city of beautiful simplicity, of impressive poverty, of concealed genius, of righteousness and exalted asceticism hidden within modest behavior, and of the simple *chesed* that is done constantly in its courtyards and alleys without anybody taking notice.

Yerushalayim of pure gold is concealed under the rough surface of people who sometimes seem cold and aloof, but who burn with the fire of humanity and *Yiddishkeit* that can be awakened by a *pashkevil* hanging on the ancient walls of the Yishuv Hayashan.

For two decades, photographer Baruch Yaari devotedly walked through the alleys of old Yerushalayim. Like a tourist whose curious soul is never satisfied, like an artist whose brush never rests, Baruch explored the land of Meah Shearim. He ate its fruits, without ever being satiated from the goodness of its people — all of its people: the righteous and the simple, the Torah geniuses and those who labored for a living, the stern characters and the friendly personalities, the poor and the rich, the kindhearted and those shattered by their journey through life. He cultivated close relationships with the elders and was careful not to annoy the younger generation.

With his unique sensitivity, Baruch blended in among the people. As if cloaked in a virtual gold-striped caftan and a flat, wide-brimmed Yerushalmi hat, he mingled with the residents, walking on tiptoes not to photograph anybody who might be offended by the photo. He memorialized special moments in time — moments that have been taking place for more than a hundred years, but that nobody had the wisdom to photograph and document until Baruch came along. Some of the moments that he documented will never occur again: their heroes have already ascended to the Meah Shearim *shel Maalah*.

The mistaken axiom that life will forever continue as is prevails in Yerushalayim. Just as the cisterns in my childhood neighborhood remain exactly where they used to be (though the community *askanim* plugged them up, leaving only their external grandeur), so too Reb Feivel Wallerstein's store at the entrance of Meah Shearim's *shuk* will forever stand. Just like the Tiger bus to the Kosel will always travel through the neighborhood's main road (which, by the way, it no longer does), so too the diligence of Rav Velvel Eisenbach will continue to echo proudly. Just as the water in Luntzer's *mikveh* will always stand, so too, those who immerse in it will live forever, and the ten measures of simple, pure human beauty that were bestowed on Meah Shearim will eternally remain.

But years have passed and Rav Feivel's store is already gone, the Tiger to the Kosel no longer passes through, Rav Velvel's *shtender* and thousands of descendants are orphaned, and some of those who immersed in Luntzer's now immerse in the Dinur River (one such special character is Rav Chaim Brim *zt"l*, who is memorialized in this work). From time to time, when the car drives through the neighborhood with loudspeakers announcing that yet another revered soul of Meah Shearim has been uprooted, everyone remembers that this life is only temporary. Then they rush to Baruch Yaari and his photographs; perhaps he succeeded in preserving some remnant of the past and memorializing it for future generations.

I, who sprouted wings and left the neighborhoods of the Yishuv Hayashan, perceive during my occasional visits that the human backdrop has changed beyond recognition. I see — and my heart shrivels within me.

•

I was a young boy in Batei Ungarin when Baruch Yaari established himself, slowly and surely, as court photographer. As a local, I noticed this frequent visitor from the big city, who was able to slip into closed events armed with a sophisticated camera, yet managed to leave without a scratch. Which "big city" was Baruch's hometown? Har Nof, but as a child of Batei Ungarin, I imagined that anything past the border of Sarei Yisrael and Shivtei Yisrael Streets was the big, outside world.

His name is not Baruch Yaari. He conceals his given name so that he cannot be identified by the people of Meah Shearim when his pictures are published in the newspapers. If they knew his real name, they would surely revoke his freedom to wander among the alleys, alleys that never saw a Canon camera since the "Chevras Bonei Yerushalayim" started building the neighborhood homes in Elul 1874.

Much has been written, said, and told over about Meah Shearim — an area that is a concept more than a neighborhood and a prototype more than a residential area. Though outsiders mistakenly think that the residents of Meah Shearim are of one mind in thought and philosophy, the truth is to the contrary.

The residents of Meah Shearim are blessed with *meah shearim* — a hundred measures — of opinions and *hashkafos*. While the conservative Perushim hasten to light the Chanukah menorah on Motza'ei Shabbos as soon as the third star has barely pierced through the heavens, the passionate Chassidim don't wish Shabbos farewell until *chatzos*. The warm, friendly approach of the few elderly Chassidei Chabad who still live in the neighborhood contrasts with the aloof zealousness of the Neturei Karta. These differences express themselves in many shapes and forms.

A stranger who might enter the *shtieblach* on the outskirts of the Meah Shearim *shuk*, behind the wall sprayed with graffiti declaring in young, clumsy handwriting that this is "Palestine," would never understand the ferocity of the disagreements that take place in its antechambers. An outsider visiting the "Hungarishe Shul" would be amazed at the colorful range of people — a vast range that includes the members of "Shuvu Banim," who live behind the Chomah Hashelishis, and ten-generation Yerushalmis, who take pride in the fact that they cannot compose a coherent sentence in modern Hebrew.

There is one common denominator between all the neighborhoods of the Yishuv Hayashan: the residents' fiercely guarded right to privacy. Most residents of the Yishuv Hayashan would react harshly, perhaps even violently (at least to the camera), at the sight of a foreign photographer documenting their lifestyle like an anthropological researcher investigating the roots of a barbarian tribe in the Amazon. The more polite residents would conceal their faces with the wide-brimmed "super" hat (some say it was created specifically for this purpose); the young and impulsive residents are likely to kick the photographer out and "take care" of his camera.

From the perspective of a Meah Shearim resident, a reaction such as this is understandable. Try walking through your neighborhood with a flock of photographers using you as a photo opp, taking pictures as you come and go, while swinging a chicken over your head for *kaparos* or inspecting the *pitom* of an esrog with a magnifying glass. Simply put, the residents of Meah

Shearim are made to feel like monkeys in the zoo — minus the bananas. The impolite photographers have only themselves to blame when they're banished.

With this background in mind, we can better appreciate Baruch Yaari's success. He went to great lengths in order to spare the residents any discomfort in his quest to document Meah Shearim. As a result, the neighborhood's leading Torah giants and personalities, whose clear wisdom and unsullied hands are unparalleled anywhere in the world, cooperated with him, trusted him, and even welcomed him into their homes. They trusted that he wouldn't photograph anything that was deemed off-limits and that his pictures wouldn't reach places that they considered inappropriate. He tiptoed through the neighborhood, as if heeding the *pashkevil* warning: Be careful, be gentle! He bent over backwards not to irritate or annoy, and made every effort not to bother or infuriate.

He tried and he succeeded.

Baruch Yaari is unique as well, in that he avoided photographing those spurned by fate and "low in mazel"; the ones with crushed hats and threadbare coats who are often chased by foolish neighborhood children — may Hashem forgive them — are not included in his repertoire of photos. He exclusively photographed Meah Shearim in all its innocence, those whose life is Torah and who walk through its alleys to their places of study, its sweet *tinokos shel beis raban*, and the way of life that cannot be found anywhere else. Those who were down on their luck and whom Meah Shearim lovingly embraced — Yaari left them to the insensitive anthropologists, to museum curators, and to those in pursuit of a Pulitzer Prize, honored with the title, "Photographers for *Chareidi* Issues."

For this accomplishment, Baruch Yaari truly deserves a Pulitzer Prize.

In 2011, Baruch merited to stand under the *chuppah*. Before closing this chapter of his life's work, he hung invitations in all the *batei midrash* in Meah Shearim: from Toldos Avraham Yitzchak to the Luntzer's Mikveh, from the Talmud Torah U'Beis Hatavshil of Toldos Aharon to those learning in Yeshuos Yaakov. He added a few handwritten lines on each invitation: "Thank you for your gracious welcome. I apologize if I unwittingly harmed someone or made someone uncomfortable when I photographed."

Years have passed since then. Baruch moved to his new home, and I also spread my wings. For me, Batei Ungarin is snippets of nostalgic memories that resurface on the Yamim Tovim and Shabbosim when I return to my homeland.

We met on Erev Sukkos 2014, when we sorted through scenes that I grew up with and magical moments that he captured with his lens, for a feature that was printed in *Mishpacha Magazine* (where I serve as Deputy Editor). We sat in front of piles of photographs that reawakened the forgotten: the glorious personalities, the curved arches, the smell of the fresh *pashkevils*, the thunder of the shoemaker's hammer in the *shuk*, and the sparks from the metalsmith's workshop across from the *shtieblach*. Little by little, this creation was born.

The article, published in a *Mishpacha* Yom Tov supplement, generated positive and enthusiastic feedback. It also inspired R' Mendy Feldheim, a man of vision and inner passion, to foresee a book published in the same format: Baruch's photos accompanied by my descriptions. After R' Mendy persistently encouraged us, we met a number of times, studied the collections and pictures, and merited to witness the luminosity of Meah Shearim *shel Maalah*. While working on this book, I relived the neighborhoods of my childhood and fell in love with them all over again. I came to the conclusion that even if outsiders disparage those who dare live life differently than they do, they cannot prevent the melody of life from playing in a neighborhood blessed with *meah shearim* — one hundred measures — of beauty.

Meah Shearim, for better or for worse, remains the heart of *chareidi* life. It is its central compass, its main artery.

First and foremost, I thank the *Borei Olam* Who, from all the places in the world, chose Batei Ungarin as the place of my birth, and me as a son to my dear parents, *mezakei harabim* and *machnisei orchim*. May Hashem bless them with a long life of goodness and well-being. My father and mother *shlita* painstakingly raised me and nurtured me among the stones of Yerushalayim and embedded Torah and *yiras Shamayim* within me. I also merited to grow up in the shadow of Rav Moshe Weber *zy"a*, the great *ohev Yisrael* and *mekarev rechokim*, whose enormous heart and humble home was open wide to every single Jew.

Even now, twenty years after his death, the influence of the Rav is a source of inspiration and vitality, providing me with needed direction at every turn. My father, Rav Ido Yitzchak Ehrlich-Weber *shlita*, continues upon the path that the Rav outlined years ago within the four magical *amos* of Batei Ungarin — devoting his life to *kiruv*, *hachnasas orchim*, and spreading the light of Torah.

A huge thank you to R' Mendy Feldheim, who was the first to think of creating this book and, with iron-willed patience and persistence, motivated, nudged, and didn't rest until he received the finished product. A heartfelt thanks to Reb Baruch Yaari for the years of faithful photography he carried out, with an artistic eye and sensitive soul, that produced this book. I hope that, *b'ezras Hashem*, additional volumes will follow.

I must express profound thanks to *Mishpacha*, the most widely read magazine among the *chareidi* public, for hosting my thoughts every week. It is within this popular platform that I merit to express my G-d-given talents as part of the elite staff of editors and writers who execute one of the most challenging jobs in the *chareidi* world: laying out a weekly magazine with features, columns, and supplements that appeal to all sectors of *chareidi* Jewry, while fastidiously guarding its sensitivities.

Thank you to publisher Eli Paley; CEO Yehudah Nachshoni; Editor in Chief Rabbi Moshe Grylak; my partner and friend in my journalistic and literary endeavors, editor Reb Yossi Elituv; secretary of the Vaad Haruchani, Rav Eliyahu Gut; Reb Yisrael Peller, who went over segments of the book, and the other talented, thoughtful members of the editorial staff. A special thanks to Reb Yossi Hausdorf, former production manager, whose mind gave birth to the first spark of the article that spawned this book.

I would like to dedicate this book to the memory of my aunt, Mrs. Ofra Rechlin *a"h*, née Wolfson (Ben-Ze'ev). She was a sixth-generation Yerushalmi, granddaughter of Gittel Dinowitz — the well-known shopkeeper from the Old City of generations past. Even after she moved during her childhood to Cairo, Egypt, and then to Tel Aviv in Gush Dan, Dodah Ofra continued to breathe its air and to tell me stories about the City of the Soul in spirited, authentic Yerushalmi Yiddish that she maintained until her very last day. She passed away on 30 Sivan 2019, old in days and years, with the many acts of *chesed* that she carried out during her lifetime escorting her on her last journey. I feel much *hakaras hatov* toward her. May the memory of Ofra bas Reb Yisrael *z"l*, a stone of the stones of Jerusalem, be blessed forever.

I invite you to walk along with Baruch Yaari and me on our remarkable journey among the stones, alleys, courtyards, moments, people, and exceptional souls of *Yerushalayim shel Maalah*.

Aryeh Ehrlich

תמונת חיי / ברוך יערי
Snapshots of My Life / Baruch Yaari

It's early in the evening and I'm sitting in my home in Givat Shaul. My children, Tamar and Shlomo, fell asleep just a few minutes ago and my wife is out teaching. A drowsy quiet spreads throughout the house and only the sound of traffic on Emek Haarazim Street attests that, for the most part, Yerushalayim is still awake.

Today, the files for the book were sent for another trial printing and, *b'ezras Hashem*, [the Hebrew] *Nishmas Yerushalayim* will soon have a physical form — pages and a binding.

I take advantage of the serenity to write an introduction and record a little bit about the life behind the photos.

My Childhood

I was born far away from the holy city of Yerushalayim, in Rechasim, a *yishuv* nestled at the foot of Mount Carmel. We had a simple, one-story house with a pleasant backyard, enhanced by three different trees: willow, *hushhash*, and lemon. The interior of my home, together with my beloved parents and eight siblings, was warm, comfortable, interesting, and always hectic.

I was a "sandwich" child who grew up with two advantages: I was involved in the lives of my older, adult siblings while I was legitimately able to have fun with the younger ones.

I still clearly remember the beautiful scenery that lay outside the window above my bed. Through the window, I could see crop duster planes gliding like birds early in the morning, above the fields of neighboring Kefar Chassidim. Their wings stirred my imagination and drew my mind up to the infinite heaven.

Our purpose as Jews in this world, descendants of the Chosen Nation that stood at the foot of Har Sinai and received the Torah, is to learn the Torah and fulfill its mitzvos. This belief was the bedrock of the home in which I was raised. At every opportunity, my father *shlita* taught us, directly and indirectly, that Yiddishkeit is not based on emotions and is certainly not anchored in temper and mood. The only thing in this world that is stable, correct, and enduring is the Torah; we live for the sake of Torah and it is our entire life. The first memories of my father are of him bending over his desk, forehead furrowed, eyes shining, and hands quickly writing on paper.

My mother transmitted to us her special way of giving to others. She embedded in us the knowledge that the *Borei Olam* wants us to do good deeds and love His creatures, and she was the embodiment of empathy, sympathy, and warmth. Our dear neighbors — Auschwitz survivors who immigrated from Romania and Hungary as well as those from Yemen, Morocco, and Tunis — were all dear to her heart. She didn't limit her *mishloach manos* containing home-baked goods to once a year; she sent them over every Erev Shabbos along with a short note expressing her genuine, warm wishes. She didn't wait for a reason or special occasion — showing interest with warm regards was reason enough to send a home-baked package.

The Yeshivah

Our house stood in the shadows of Yeshivah Knesses Chizkiyahu. The yeshivah was the cornerstone of the *yishuv*, and all the homes were built around it. We, in particular, lived in close proximity to it. At the time, the great Roshei Yeshivah still walked on the narrow, village paths, and the structures — copies of the *batei midrash* of Slobodka, Mir, and Kelm — were still standing. We sometimes davened in the ancient edifice that still reverberated with the *sichos mussar* of the Lev Eliyahu, Rav Eliyahu Lopian *zt"l*, after whom I am named.

The personality that most affected my childhood was "The Mashgiach," Rav Dov Yaffe *zt"l*. He personified outer and inner splendor. His internal life was rooted in his *rebbeim* and their *rebbeim* of generations past, in the yeshivah world of Europe before the War. His large eyes were always reflective, and expressed humility, purity, and love, both when he stood at the *bimah* next to the Aron Kodesh delivering an inspirational *shmuess*, encouraging us to grow in *mussar*, and when I stood in the long line together with everybody else on Friday night to wish him a *gut Shabbos*.

My Youth

We definitely didn't learn art in *cheder*. The Talmud Torah encouraged us to spend our free time learning the *Shishah Sidrei Mishnah* by heart, word for word, in order to be tested on it. I do have fond memories, however, of my seventh-grade rebbe, R' Yigal Ganut, who taught us *Maseches Eiruvin*. He helped us create miniature courtyards and lanes made of cardboard — "*chatzeiros*" and "*mevo'os*;" "*pasei beira'os*" and "*reshus harabim*." I sat for hours after *cheder* building these artistic creations. Regrettably, I wasn't smart enough to save them.

During a different period of time, I spent many evenings sitting in the yeshivah library, summarizing *masechtos* of *mishnayos* on long, narrow pieces of paper that I then pasted together to create lengthy reels. Right before my bar mitzvah, I began learning in Yeshivah Keren Orah of Rav Tzvi Margalit, Rav of Karmiel, which is located in the Galilee Mountains. The Rosh Yeshivah, Rav Tzvi Blatt *shlita*, taught me how to toil over the *peshat* in the *sugya* by delving into the words of Rashi. When it became time to move on to Yeshivah Gedolah, I moved to Yerushalayim to study in Torah Ohr, the yeshivah of Maran HaRav HaGaon Chaim Pinchas Scheinberg *zt"l*, whose genius, *hasmadah*, *tzidkus,* and warmth serve as a model of the perfect blend of *yirah* and *ahavah* until today.

By the end of the summer *zeman*, most of my siblings were already learning in yeshivos in Yerushalayim, so my dear parents fulfilled their dream of returning to live in the Holy City where their life together had first begun.

The roots of my family, both on my father's and mother's sides, are deeply embedded in Yerushalayim.

My paternal grandparents, Rav Shmuel Yeshayahu Greenwald *zt"l* and his wife, settled in Batei Warsaw after they moved from Poland, and the extended Greenwald family from the Breslov Shul in Meah Shearim are cousins of my father.

On my mother's side, my grandmother's father was the *Darchei Dovid*, Rav Mordechai Dovid Levin *zt"l*, Rosh Yeshivah of Etz Chaim. When the elderly Yerushalmis hear his name, they still tremble reverently. (I once mentioned my grandfather to Rav Zundel Kroizer; he immediately stood up and, with a nostalgic look, said, "He was my rebbe.")

His son-in-law, my dear righteous grandfather, was Rav Yaakov Moshe Korlandski *zt"l*. He founded Yavneh, the first Litvish *cheder*; many of today's Roshei Yeshivah were his *talmidim*.

We left the small *yishuv* of Rechasim and moved to the large *Ir Hakodesh*, Yerushalayim. I continued learning in Yeshivah Torah Ohr in Mattersdorf while my home was in Har Nof. I loved the learning in the yeshivah, the yeshivah atmosphere, and the merit of sitting in the presence of *talmidei chachamim* who glowed with the light of Torah and illuminated those who sat in their shadows.

For various reasons, I later left the yeshivah with a heavy heart, but I never said goodbye to it.

The Birth of Nishmas Yerushalayim

I had a camera and was looking for something to photograph — something with deep significance...

I once came to take pictures in the Mishkenos Haroim Shul on Meah Shearim Street, and it was there that I saw "Reb Leibish" for the very first time. Hesitantly, I moved closer with the camera. He lifted his head, gave me a penetrating look — a look suffused with love that was uniquely his — and, without a word, granted me permission to photograph him. He then dove back into the Gemara by peering through a magnifying glass, the handle faded and rubbed away from constant use, held in a hand that was wrinkled with the passage of time and life experiences.

At that moment I felt an inexplicable bond to the man and his neighborhood and everything that his appearance represented.

That bond never faded.

I never left Reb Leibish. I came back many times, until the day that I arrived to photograph him in the Ba'al Hatanya Shul, located in the *shuk*. I saw him walking towards the shul, but when I returned a few minutes later, when he should have already started the *shiur*, I found a tumult at the entrance to the shul. No sooner had Reb Leibish placed his hand on the door handle than his life song came to an abrupt end. Later, when I visited his brother, the elderly Reb Yeshayah, I told him about my relationship with Reb Leibish and that I wanted to hear more about him. He gave me a humble look unique to elderly Yerushalmis, and said, "The relationship that you had with my brother, you can continue with me."

His astonished grandson couldn't understand why his grandfather, a *mashgiach* in the Satmar yeshivah and a passionate *kanai*, allowed a photographer to wander around taking pictures at will. Reb Yeshayah explained that with a "friend" the rules are different...

The bond that an old man has with the Gemara that he studied throughout his life is one of deep, burning love. This love is mostly hidden, but at times it could be glimpsed on Reb Yeshayah's face, and sometimes even seen in his fingers that held the Gemara.

I always tried to capture this love in my photos.

At times, I believe I succeeded.

Over time, I became acquainted with more personalities of the Meah Shearim community; its *talmidei chachamim*, *masmidim*, laborers and, of course, the pure, charming children who played in its alleys.

Thank you, Hashem, for making sure that I met good people who guided me to the *"yakirei Yerushalayim,"* the Yerushalayim nobility, and for the interesting situations that I encountered in the neighborhoods. The favor in which I was perceived by some of the most unique Yerushalmi personalities, and the fact that they opened their homes to me at all times, was a special, Heaven-sent *chesed*.

Rav and Rebbetzin Kuperstock in the Batei Broide neighborhood opened their doors to me, treated me like their own son, and showered me with love, *berachos,* and *tefillos*.

There was no distinction between their *"kodesh"* and *"chol"* activities: Both comprised one solid unit of love for Hashem and His creations. The Rav would shed tears as he threw food to the birds just as he let the tears flow while reciting *Tehillim* non-stop on Fridays. The same way he was submerged in the *sugya* of electricity on Shabbos — a subject discussed at length in one of his *sefarim* — he invested his all when decorating the shul with magnificent *"lemplach"* (oil holders). The

Rebbetzin davened next to her boiling pot of fish on Erev Shabbos with the same *d'veikus* as she davened, snuggled in a blanket against the Yerushalayim cold, next to the Chanukah candles.

Once, while visiting their home during the Second Lebanon War, I found the Rebbetzin to be quite distraught. Though newspapers or media of any sort never entered their home, someone had informed her that the soldiers had entered the battlefield without having even rolls to eat. Oy, how she cried for them!

There was an indescribable, mutual admiration between the Rav and the Rebbetzin. The Rebbetzin was a quintessential queen; I have never seen such adoration of a wife towards her husband anywhere else in the world. When the Rav sat and learned at the long table in their living room — which also served as their bedroom — she sat across from him at the other end of the table, watching him with pure admiration. The Rav was an unusually quiet person, and they had an unwritten agreement: he would speak words of *divrei Torah* for her, and she would speak of all other matters in his stead.

When I came to invite them to my wedding, they were both quite old and living with their daughter. The Rav listened with pleasure while resting in his bed, but didn't join the conversation at all. A minute before I left, he opened his mouth and said three words: "*Levater, levater, levater*" (Give in, give in, give in). The next time I visited, it was to be *menachem avel* the Rebbetzin. She accepted the Heavenly judgment, but had one question: How can one take a Sefer Torah and bury it in the ground?

THE HEART OF THE BOOK

Looking through the book, readers will notice that there are barely any pictures of women. Those familiar with the nuances and sensitivities of Meah Shearim don't need an explanation for this omission; even so, I will try to explain the reasoning behind this decision. I desperately want the people of Meah Shearim to embrace this book, bond with it, and be proud of it.

In Meah Shearim, women are treasured diamonds, guarded with great reserve. In this context, publicity tarnishes the splendor of a pure diamond. After so many years of cultivating a loving, respectful relationship with the good people of Meah Shearim, I won't do anything that would insult them.

I took pictures of the children of Yerushalayim at almost every opportunity. These children are graced with a special charm, and the spark of joy and love of life is easily seen in their eyes. I don't speak or understand Yiddish, so I've often wondered if more doors would have opened if I did. On the other hand, perhaps I was able to perceive more details within the simplest things because I don't speak or understand it.

One picture is worth a thousand words, but there are some concepts that a picture cannot express without the power of words. The thoughts of the heart, the feelings hidden deep within the soul of the people of Meah Shearim can only be described with words. Nobody can do this better than Aryeh Ehrlich.

Reb Aryeh grew up in the alleys of Meah Shearim and the courtyards of Batei Ungarin. His writing is serious and steeped with *yiras Shamayim*, yet mixed with a mischievous sense of humor. Most of all, he writes with sensitivity and tact, and perfectly describes the internal life of the residents of Meah Shearim.

I didn't know Aryeh as a child, but I photographed him a number of times within the neighborhood, and he appears in one of the pictures in this book.

THANK YOU

Thank you to the Rosh Yeshivah of Sha'arei Yosher, Rav Moshe Goldstein *shlita*. I was a *talmid* in his yeshivah for close to a decade during the twenty years that I spent photographing in Meah Shearim. The Rav helped guide me along the right path that enabled Baruch Yaari's photography in Meah Shearim to merge with Eliyahu Greenwald's personal and spiritual life. For this, I owe him my life.

Thank you to the Rosh Yeshivah of Derech Hashem, Rav Tzvi Greenbaum *shlita*, whose yeshivah hosted me during the second decade of my Meah Shearim photography, as a *talmid* and, until today, an alumnus. I think that this work embodies the unique *derech Hashem* taught in the yeshivah. This is expressed on the yeshivah wall that bears an exhibition of some photos that I took of workmen in Meah Shearim.

Thank you to Rina Hollander of the *New York Times*, the first person to notice the special angle in my photos and encourage me to focus on Meah Shearim.

A special thanks to photographer Ittay Bodell, whose professional hands greatly improved the quality of these pictures. Thank you to Mrs. Esther Bezalel for designing this book and investing her many talents in it. She gave much more time and effort than she was compensated for, and she never gave up on the project, even though it took years to finish (a special thanks to her husband for this as well). Thanks to Mrs. Tehilah Goldbaum from Esther's studio for her dedicated work and the design aspect of the book.

A special thank you to R' Mendy Feldheim, who never gave up, though we worked on this book for more than ten years. He approached the project with his trademark energy and love of life, and relentlessly set one new deadline after the next for publishing the book. Without his strong *emunah* in the Creator, integral optimism, and perseverance, the book would have never been published.

Thank you to all who were my partners in this lengthy journey, beginning when I took my very first photos. It is impossible to list them all, because there are too many — especially my friends and acquaintances in Meah Shearim.

Thank you to my employer, whose name testifies to its essence, loyalty, and integrity: the *Yated Neeman*, which has presented my pictures for close to twenty years.

Thank you to the CEO, Rav Zelig Orlansky; Chief Editor, Rav Yisrael Friedman; and the editor of the weekly *Yated*, Rav Avraham Rosenthal. Thank you to the coordinators and producers who work behind the scenes to make the *Yated* what it is, Mrs. Chana Gorel and Mrs. Penina Ginzburg, and to all the writers, who are too many to list.

There is one exceptionally talented writer who I must mention — my beloved older brother, Rav Shmuel Greenwald. Working together as field correspondents, we were hosted by Bedouins in Kasif and by Druze at Mt. Hermon. We investigated cemeteries and old archives in kibbutzim, crouched together in fields outside of Gaza while mortars flew above us, and curled up in the bottom of a car lost in the alleys of Ramallah.

Thank you to my beloved parents for leading me along my path.

Thank you to my dear wife, my partner in the solid Jewish home that we built together. On our very first date, I brought printed sketches of the first version of this book. Since then, she has been waiting patiently along with me to see it published.

More than anything, thank you to the *Borei Olam* for His tremendous *chesed* and compassion, and for the special path which He paved for me.

I daven that the book will find favor in the eyes of the Creator and mankind.

Baruch Yaari

נשמת ירושלים

The Soul of Yerushalayim

> **He was a Jew of light. Every Erev Shabbos, he prepared the lamps in his home and in the Batei Broide shul in honor of the Shabbos Queen.**
>
> ("A Jew of Light," page 19)

CHAPTER ONE

Shabbos

יהודי של אור
A Jew of Light

Rav Yitzchak Nosson Kuperstock had a special affinity for the mitzvah of lighting lamps. He channeled his energy into *hadlakas neiros*: Shabbos lamps, Chanukah flames, and the Lag Ba'Omer fire. He was a Jew of light. Every Erev Shabbos, he prepared the lamps in his home and in the Batei Broide shul in honor of the Shabbos Queen. Standing on a ladder, he polished the oil lamps, prepared the wicks, and poured oil into the glasses.

When Baruch Yaari asked if he could photograph him, the *gaon* of Batei Broide answered with charming humility, "If you enjoy it, here I am. Take pictures at will. If you want me to move, tell me and I'll move wherever you want." He was a man of *chesed*, and if he could help another *Yid* with *parnassah*, he waived his own prestige and honor so that he could help.

Rav Yitzchak Nosson's flames never flickered. They were always straight, and ascended upward serenely. They reflected his own soul, his own *ner neshamah*, which was also serene and illuminated by a halo. The halo was that of a Yerushalmi *gaon* who diligently studied Torah, who was meticulous with his every action, and who knew that his life's achievements were packed and ready for the day that his *neshamah* would reconnect to its Eternal Source.

Here he is in his home, preparing the lamps in honor of Shabbos. Behind him is an old refrigerator with an even older, broken fan on top of it, because this world is only an antechamber leading to the World to Come.

ירָאה עילאה

Yirah Ila'ah

Reb Yeshaya Deutsch *zt"l*, referred to as "Reb Shayeh," was as solid as an ancient stone within the curved arch above the entrance of the Meah Shearim courtyard. Purity radiated from his face, an aura of sanctity matched his white beard, and an inspired antiquity rested above his doubled yarmulke. Out of *yiras Shamayim*, he never learned Torah without two large head coverings, one on top of the other, that covered most of his head: one for *Yirah Ila'ah* and the second for *Yirah Tata'ah*.

Reb Shayeh was a "*Yehudi shel Maalah*." He lived in Batei Warsaw, behind the Perushim Shul. Every Erev Shabbos, he sat on a bench in his cluttered kitchen, next to the "*sarateh*" — the two layers of tablecloth that covered his table. Face shining with joy, he delved into the Mishnah Berurah and then poured olive oil into the special holders.

When Baruch Yaari told him that he merited to have a special relationship with Reb Leibish, his brother who had recently passed away, Reb Shayeh looked at him and said, "The relationship that you had with my brother, you can continue with me."

The friendship did continue. The bond was maintained until the day that Reb Shayeh joined Reb Leibish in the *Yeshivah shel Maalah*, where, we can imagine, they both sit and prepare the lamps.

זכור ושמור

Remember the Shabbos Day

Rav Avraham Yaakov Epstein *zt"l* was a leader of the Neturei Karta, as well as a soldier in its battles. Although he was born in South America and didn't imbibe Yerushalmi zealousy in his infancy, he became a veteran *kanai*. He marched in protests and was the spokesman during the sackcloth-and-ash rallies on Yom Haatzmaut.

Every year, on the night of Tishah B'Av, when Jews lament the destruction of the Beis HaMikdash, Rav Avraham Yaakov took up his post next to the Meah Shearim *shtieblach*. He stood on a table that the Neturei Karta youth dragged from the Hadar candy store, sweat of the mitzvah streaming down their faces. During the rest of the year, the table was used to sell sweets, but on Tishah B'Av, it was used to decry the spiritual breaches of the generation.

Rav Avraham Yaakov's voice thundered across the entire Meah Shearim. The megaphone intensified his protest so that the whole Eretz Hakodesh would tremble. After all, Chazal warned that if one does not protest the sinful breaches for which the generation is punished, he also will be punished for their sins.

Rav Epstein had another *minhag*: The minute that *L'chu Neranenah* in the *Yom* song for Wednesday was said at the end of Shacharis, he would go through the markets of Geulah and Machaneh Yehudah, hanging "*tzetlach*" on the stores. These small notices announced the time that Shabbos would begin that week, as it says, "*Zachor es yom haShabbos l'kadsho.*" The merchants in the *shuk* greeted him with a smile because they knew that he was a man of truth, who feared Hashem and sincerely valued Shabbos.

החלות של לנדנר
Lendner's Challah

Lendner's Challah — there was nothing like it in the entire world.

For 124 years, the bakery stood on Rav Leib Dayan Street in the Beis Yisrael neighborhood, behind the neighborhood *shtieblach*. Only fragrant Shabbos challah was baked here; to taste this challah, especially on Friday night, was to taste Gan Eden. On Thursdays, people came from far and wide, even people whose walk and talk was very different than the walk and talk of Meah Shearim, in order to buy the challah that would honor Shabbos.

Yerushalayim epicures maintain that Lendner's Challah can only be found at Lendner; all imitations are doomed to fail.

Matisyahu Lendner was an eminent third-generation challah baker. The secrets of the challah were guarded safely in his mind, as secure as the secret recipe of Coca-Cola, known only to the management — and to Rav Landau, who gives its *hashgachah* in Eretz Yisrael, of course.

When people asked about the secret of the Lendner challah, he answered, "Every week, when I knead the dough and braid the challah, I sing *'L'kavod Shabbos Kodesh, L'kavod Shabbos Kodesh.'* That is why the challah comes out so good." Was this his way of evading the answer, or did he truly believe in his statement? We'll never know.

All types visited the bakery: *chareidim* and those who weren't, Jews and non-Jews, simple people alongside ministers and princes. The price of a single challah wasn't cheap, but the expenses of Shabbos aren't included in our budget anyway. Those who take pleasure in Shabbos have boundless wealth, and there is no better way to enjoy Shabbos than by making a *Hamotzi* on Friday night on a fragrant Lendner challah.

I was once hosted for a Shabbos in Antwerp, Belgium, on condition that I bring a gift of fresh Lendner challah. On Thursday night, I walked to the bakery and reverently wrapped the fragrant challah that accompanied me over the Mediterranean Sea. I pitied the custom officials in Brussels whose Belgian propriety prevented them from pulling off a piece of the intoxicating, aromatic challah and popping it into their mouths. Their politeness saved the challah for my Antwerpian friend.

Here is Reb Zusha Gorelitz, the legendary baker, braiding the challah in the Lendner Bakery while his lips murmur *"L'kavod Shabbos Kodesh."*

In Iyar 2019, the bakery closed, leaving masses of Jews yearning for the Shabbos taste of Lendner challah.

האגדה לבית בריזל

The Legend of Beit Brizel

At the entrance to Meah Shearim Street stands the Brizel Bakery, which specializes in yeast cakes, "*lekach*" balls, and other baked goods upon which generations have been raised. The baked goods are eaten without guilt, and even with gusto, because in Meah Shearim there is little to no awareness about nutrition. What's important is to eat until one is satiated, *l'shem Shamayim*, of course, in order to have energy to serve the Creator. On Shabbos, one should utter "*l'kavod Shabbos Kodesh*" with great *kavanah* in order to assuage his conscience.

The bakery is owned by Rav Berish Brizel, a Pinsk-Karlin Chassid (an "*Alte Karliner*"). He is a *mechutan* of the Admor of Pinsk-Karlin and the patriarch of a magnificent Yerushalmi family. His great acts of kindness are numerous, yet known by no one.

The bakery is not only a source of income, but his life's work. Though he has many employees, Rav Berish is *mafrish challah* by himself and prepares the challah in honor of Shabbos. When the challah is ready (with *challah* taken per halachah), braided for Shabbos or rounded for Yom Tov, he sprinkles sesame seeds liberally while simultaneously murmuring that his challah baking is performed in honor of the Shabbos Queen.

דגים לכבוד שבת
Fish in Honor of Shabbos

The people of Yerushalayim make sure to eat fish every Friday night, as the popular saying goes: One who eats *"dag"* (fish — דג) on the day of *"dag"* (seventh day, as seven is the total numerical value of 4+3 [ד+ג]), will be saved from *"dag"* (the judgment of Gehinnom — initials of ד"ג] דין גיהנום]).

Those who glorify the mitzvah shop at Rosner's fish store. Yerushalmis prefer carp because its whiteness and taste make gefilte fish balls worthy enough for Shabbos. Some maintain that carp's cheap price is the main advantage because, although rich in wisdom, the people of Yerushalayim are generally poor in wealth.

The children often stop at Rosner's store on their way home from *cheder* to observe the fish as they calmly swim in a large tub of water. The elders tell the fascinated children, "Look at these fish that cannot live outside of water, and learn a lesson: we too cannot live without water, as water is Torah."

The Rosner brothers expertly cut and prepare the fish. The Yerushalmi notables, the lofty people who have nothing in their world other than *kedushah* and *taharah*, stand in line and concentrate deeply while they wait for their fish. They daven to receive a good fish, with regard to its taste as well as for the *gilgul neshamah* within it, because the *neshamos* of tzaddikim come back in the form of fish in order to receive their *tikkun* when served at the Shabbos tables of pious Jews.

Others take advantage of the waiting time to learn from a *sefer*, as did Rav Avraham Yaakov Epstein. His image, memorialized in this picture, testifies to his maximization of time.

ריח מגן־עדן
The Fragrance of Gan Eden

Rav Nachman Lutzkin of the "Shtetlach" was the crowning glory of the Nachlaot landscape. The neighborhood resembles an old-fashioned painting, Rav Nachman as a picture within it.

Everyone's attention is drawn to him when he walks through the *shuk* because of his *hadras panim*, the passion in his eyes, refined appearance, purity of character, and other myriad traits. The savvy Yerushalmis have referred to Rav Nachman as a stone of Yerushalayim humanity, a main artery of its vitality, and one of its thousands of impressive hues.

Rav Nachman Lutzkin during the workdays of the week is nothing like the Rav Nachman Lutzkin on Erev Shabbos. On Friday, he blends into the masses of Yerushalmis in the Machaneh Yehudah *shuk* who fill their baskets in honor of the Shabbos Queen.

The shopkeepers' boisterous shouting of "Only today!" "Take advantage today, tomorrow will be too late!" to promote their wares fills the *shuk* with a mix of deafening voices as Rav Nachman walks through. (The *melamdim* in Yerushalayim tell their rowdy students, "Zeit shtil, s'iz nisht Machaneyuda du — Be quiet, this is not Machaneh Yehudah!")

Rav Nachman is here for a purpose: to buy *besamim* in honor of Shabbos. He looks just like the person carrying bundles of myrtle branches who encountered Rabbi Shimon bar Yochai and Rabbi Elazar when they left the cave in Pekiin for the second time. Then, the tzaddikim were *melamed zechus* on the entire world in the merit of the old man who honored Shabbos with his bundles of myrtle; so too, Rav Nachman brings merits to the world and draws Divine compassion through the *besamim* that he buys in the *shuk*.

On Friday night, he walks between the people in shul and offers them the *zechus* of reciting *borei minei besamim*. Though this is a Sephardi custom — the Ashkenazim generally prefer "*a shmek tabak*" (mint- or bazooka-flavored snuff) — Rav Nachman deemed it a worthy *minhag* and adopted it as his own.

As he sings the words of the Arizal, "*bechamra go chasa, umedanei asa,*" he draws the smell of the myrtles into his lungs as his *neshamah yeseirah* delights in the fragrance of Gan Eden.

סוד המרצפות העתיקות
The Secret of the Ancient Tiles

Batei Neitin is a picturesque neighborhood. Two short, arched tunnels cross its length and an antiquated architectural design places homes above the tunnels to maximize residential space.

Batei Neitin's shul is located above one of these tunnels. The neighborhood's G-d-fearing residents wake up early and retire to bed late, filling their time with Torah and *tefillah*. They cloak themselves in armor, impervious to the modern world and its foreign ideas, so that their purity remains unscathed.

The floor tiles of this ancient shul have never been replaced and the wide chinks between them make cleaning difficult. Nevertheless, the residents of Batei Neitin maintain their belief that these tiles have absorbed one hundred years of *kedushah* and therefore cannot be replaced. The effort put into cleaning them is more than worthwhile because it preserves the glory of previous years. If "the walls of a person testify about him," the same must be true of the floor tiles in shul.

Many notable people davened in this shul, including Rav Aharon Krull *zt"l*, a sharp Polish Chassid who basked in the shadow of the Beis Yisrael of Gur *zt"l*; Rav Uri Weinberger *zt"l*, known for his exemplary *hachnasas orchim*; and many other people of spiritual grandeur.

In this picture, you can see the shul's *shamash*, Rav Moshe Nachum Friedman, a Meah Shearim *talmid chacham*, arranging benches in honor of the Shabbos Queen. Next to him is Reb Leizer Hershler, an *ish chesed* who invites all the poor and homeless people into his home and sukkah, reading *shnayim mikra v'echad targum*.

בְּחַגְוֵי הַסֶּלַע

My Dove, in the Clefts of the Rock

Rav Yitzchak Nosson Kuperstock was a Yerushalmi *gaon*. His eyes were deep and penetrating and his essence radiated simple, serene *yiras haromemus*. He lived in Batei Broide, and every morning he davened Shacharis *k'vasikin*.

Before his own breakfast, he would take a bowl and toss crumbs to the birds. When the birds chirped in front of him, tears of joy would appear in the corners of his eyes. His happiness was generated by observing the living things Hashem created and by the privilege of feeding them, thereby cleaving to the ways of the Creator, Who sustains and nourishes all — from *karnei reimim* to *beitzei kinim*.

As he fed the birds, his lips whispered and murmured holy words. Perhaps these were murmurs of *tefillah*, perhaps *limud haTorah*, or perhaps something else entirely — something that drew him closer to his Creator. Great *yeshuos* were seen there, for those who were *zocheh*.

I imagine him telling the *Ribbono shel Olam*: Just as the compassion of the mother bird is stirred for her young chicks, You too, with Your infinite compassion, guard Your fledglings — the Jewish people — as it says in Your Torah, "[Hashem is] like an eagle that awakens its nest, and hovers over its young."

מה יפו פעמיך
How Beautiful Are Your Feet in Shoes

Lofty secrets are concealed in the act of polishing shoes on Erev Shabbos. I don't know these secrets, but they're revealed to *yerei Shamayim* who have a reason for everything that they do. On Erev Shabbos, these *Yidden* go outside with polish and brush and reverently polish their shoes in honor of Shabbos.

In Yerushalayim, there is a systematic method for shining one's shoes: First and foremost, the polish must be a solid paste kept in a tin container. This paste is smeared on the shoe for the first round of polishing, which is followed by a second round of polishing and brushing that leaves the shoe shining in honor of Shabbos.

After the rubbing and polishing, the shoes are left to dry. Meanwhile, wearing "*fantufel*" (slippers), the shoe owners trim their nails and arrange their "*mikveh-tosh*" (*mikveh* bag), as they prepare to immerse in the purifying waters of the neighborhood *mikveh*.

בנהר דינור
The Dinur River

On Erev Shabbos, the Yerushalmi elders go to the *mikveh* after *chatzos* in honor of the Shabbos Queen. Their hands hold a bag with their white clothes and their faces shine with a splendid *kedushah*. They usually walk without a hat because anything that isn't needed at the *mikveh* is better left at home where there are less chances of it getting lost. This is, therefore, the only opportunity to see these *Yidden*, who are always careful about *Yirah Ila'ah* and *Yirah Tata'ah* reflected in their double head coverings, walking on the street with only a yarmulke on their heads.

These elders of the Yishuv concentrate on many "*kavanos*" as they immerse. Some immerse four times, parallel to the four directions; others immerse thirteen times, corresponding to the thirteen *middos shel rachamim*; and some immerse twenty-six times, corresponding to the numerical equivalent of *Hakadosh Baruch Hu*'s ineffable Name.

After immersing, they dry themselves off with saintly intent, as if they have just immersed in the Dinur River, known to purify all spiritual stains. There are those who concentrate on curing the sick and drawing down salvation to this world, like Rebbe Shlomke of Zhvill *zy"a*. When he received names for *yeshuah* and sage advice for serious and complicated situations, he would immerse while concentrating on the names. When he ascended, his answers were prepared, and powerful salvation waited for those in need.

התנאה לפניו בפֵאות

Beautifying the *Peyos*

Yerushalmis take great pride in their carefully arranged and neatly curled *peyos*. There are those who hide their *peyos* behind their ears, underneath their yarmulke, curled up tight, or cut short; in Yerushalayim, the longer and curlier the *peyos*, the better. After all, *peyos* are the sign of the Jewish people, who observe the mitzvah of *lo sakifu* and beautify it, as with all mitzvos.

From the age of three until their death (or until their hair falls out), Yerushalmis cultivate their *peyos* because it signifies that they are the children of Avraham, Yitzchak, and Yaakov, who are "merciful, G-d-fearing, and charitable." Moreover, the *peyos* proudly defy the conventions of the external world and unabashedly challenge those who proclaim themselves free of mitzvah performance, and are wont to poke fun at the authentic Jewish appearance.

Over time, various techniques have been developed and used to curl *peyos*. In Yerushalayim, however, sprays and shpritzes and the like are rarely used. Instead, the curls are made with the same techniques used by their forefathers in the Yishuv Hayashan — as you can see in these pictures.

מזהירין על השבת

Keep the Shabbos Day

"**M**azhirei HaShabbos," those who give warning of Shabbos's imminent arrival, walk around Shuk Machaneh Yehudah before Shabbos spreads its wings over Yerushalayim and encourage the shopkeepers to close their shutters.

They do this faithfully, week after week, after a lengthy walk from Meah Shearim. There's no need to speak or protest; a Shabbos trumpet and *shtreimel* are sufficient. The merchants usually take the hint and immediately lower their prices, for after all, the man with the trumpet is here already.

Recalcitrant storekeepers receive special treatment. The "*mazhir haShabbos*" stands at the entrance of the store and blasts loudly with his trumpet, until the storekeeper has no other choice but to shut his shop.

When his work is done, the *mazhir haShabbos* then goes to welcome the Shabbos, happy and satisfied that he merited to save others from *chillul Shabbos*. When he arrives back in his neighborhood, he sees the elderly walking with towels on their heads and *mikveh* bags under their arms, having added extra purity to their purity by immersing in the waters of Luntzer's Mikveh in Meah Shearim.

פעקעלע לכבוד שבת

Pekeleh in Honor of Shabbos

The children of the Yishuv Hayashan wait for Erev Shabbos, when their *peyos* will be curled after a warm bath, and wearing a white shirt and Shabbos vest, they'll walk to shul "*Shabbosdik*." In shul, they'll meet their friends, join the crowd of those davening with *d'veikus*, and see the sacred *avodah* of the Rebbe from up close.

There is no greater joy in the world than the joy of a "*Shabbosdik*" Yerushalmi child in shul holding a Shabbos *pekeleh* filled with snacks that his mother prepared for him.

דור לדור יביעו

One Generation to the Next

The bond between generations in the Yishuv Hayashan is stronger than anywhere else in the world. The people of Yerushalayim are characterized by their pure innocence. Even in old age, they are swathed in childlike purity, like a baby who hasn't yet tasted sin, because they haven't let the outer world invade their private *dalet amos*.

The basis of communication in the traditional Yerushalayim communities is strictly intergenerational: a father's communication to his son, grandfather to grandson, and great-grandfather to great-grandson. That's why when the people of Yerushalayim sit amongst their progeny — third and fourth generation — there's no difference between the *yiras Shamayim* of the grandfather and that of the grandson. The only difference is in their age.

Of all the threads that bind grandfathers to their grandsons, there is nothing stronger and deeper than the page of Gemara that the grandfather in Yerushalayim learns with his grandson, who devoutly follows his path.

Seventy or eighty years ago, the grandfather looked exactly the way his grandson looks now. The same will be true of his grandson's grandson: in another seventy or eighty years, he too will look exactly the same.

ויבוא גוי צדיק

The Righteous Nation

Friday night, the fifth of Sivan 2012. The day had been long and replete with Shavous preparations, and my body yearned for a bit of rest. But inside the Shomrei Emunim Beis Midrash, it was light as day.

It was two o'clock in the morning. The Rebbe entered the *beis midrash*, his face aflame, eyes closed, and beard gleaming. "*Yom hashishi, vayichili hashumayim*," the senior Admor of the generation began to chant.

It was the last Kiddush of his life...

Three o'clock in the morning. The world slumbers. All lie on their beds. Only in that *beis midrash* with the high ceiling, marble-covered walls, and gold Aron Kodesh is it light as day.

The Rebbe sits, his fervent face ablaze like the sun glowing during sunset. Soon, after the soup, he'll begin "*Kah Ribon*" in the heartrending melody composed by his father, Rebbe Arele Roth zy"a, author of *Taharas Hakodesh*. As he sings this holy melody, the hardest heart begins to melt. His eyes close and he ascends. His deep, penetrating, gentle voice soars high and joins the *malachim*.

The day after Yom Tov, following a long life of *avodas hakodesh*, his heart stops. He doesn't recover and, on the fifth of Elul 2012, he ascends to the *Yeshivah shel Maalah*.

The Rebbe of Shomrei Emunim zt"l was a tzaddik and *parush*, who was simultaneously disconnected from the physical world and its people, yet the very heart of the nation.

He wasn't afraid to share his opinion: He defined a recent president of the United States as "a dog sent by the forces of impurity." He viewed the expulsion of the Jews from Gush Katif as a deadly sin and spoke about the curse that will befall those who promoted it. He dedicated his days and nights to *tefillah* for Am Yisrael.

Each of his four sons took over for his father in his own locale, but truthfully, nobody could take over the Rebbe's position. His position was high and lofty, at times even mysterious and implausible to the regular human mind. He was a vestige of the Rebbes of generations back, who left orphaned congregations when they ascended to the Heavens.

בספינקא בוערת אש
A Fire Burns in Spinka

Admor Mordechai Dovid Kahana of Spinka *zt"l* was a remarkable personality and a link in the unbroken chain of *Kehunah* from the days of the Beis HaMikdash. When I was thirty days old, my father dropped five silver coins into his hand to redeem me according to halachah. I was brought to the Chassidish shul in Batei Ungarin and adorned by the neighborhood women with gold chains and valuable jewelry. The Rebbe asked my father what he preferred: his son or five coins. Luckily, my father chose me.

At that critical moment, it was discovered that in all of the hullabaloo, the five coins had been left at home. My father ran home to retrieve them; otherwise, I could have become a "Spinker Einekel"....

Whenever I encountered the famous Rebbe, I reminded him that I had merited to be redeemed by him. He always responded with a warm *berachah*, recited in the unique melody of higher and lower tones he used while saying *divrei Torah* and speaking with people.

"In Spinka *brent* a fire — A fire burns in Spinka." That's what they used to say in this special Chassidus. The fire was a fire of *avodas Hashem*, the fire of Torah, and the fire of *ahavas Yisrael*, all found in the Rebbe's radiant presence. Here he sits on Motza'ei Shabbos, a warm drink in front of him, as he records *chiddushei Torah* that took shape over Shabbos.

חמין במוצאי שבת

Escorting the Shabbos Queen

It is impossible to describe the *kedushah* that surrounded Rav Avraham Yaakov Zeleznik *zt"l*, Rosh Yeshivah of Etz Chaim, as he escorted the Shabbos Queen out from his austere and simple home with lit candles and a hot drink. Week after week, following an exalted Shabbos of *hasmadah*, the walls of his home in the Kerem neighborhood watched as he closed his eternal Gemara in order to prepare for the meal of Dovid Hamelech.

Rav Avraham Yaakov lived in his "temporary dwelling" for ninety-eight years, his only acquisition in *Olam Hazeh*. For ninety-eight years, he elevated himself until he achieved true greatness. In addition to his genius, good *middos*, the thousands of *talmidim* whom he taught, and his involvement in the community, his dedication to the mitzvah of *Melaveh Malkah* was inspirational.

ניחוח של תחיית המתים

Scent of *Techiyas Hameisim*

The *Melaveh Malkah seudah* is cherished by *yerei Shamayim*, Chassidim and *perushim* alike. Together they sit by lit candles and escort the Shabbos out with song and praise, stories of tzaddikim, prayers for a successful week, references to Dovid Hamelech, and the story of Eliyahu Hanavi, who sold himself and constructed a building overnight in order to provide sustenance for the *ish chasid bli mazon u'michya*.

The menu is usually sparse. It primarily consists of Shabbos leftovers and boiling-hot soup with kneidlach, all prepared by volunteers. The soup is an important component, as our Sages taught us that a hot drink on Motza'ei Shabbos is a medicinal tonic. In the *Yishuv Hayashan*, the sparsity of material food at the *Melaveh Malkah* is accompanied by an abundance of spirituality.

A holy fragrance is present: the scent of *techiyas hameisim*. As Chazal says, the Luz bone, from which a person will be resurrected during *techiyas hameisim*, is nourished by the *seudah* of *Melaveh Malkah*.

סעודתא דדוד מלכא
Seudasa d'Dovid Malka

Sweetness reigns in the Chassidish shul in Batei Rand, named after Reb Menachem Mendel Rand, where Chassidim gather on Motza'ei Shabbos within its ancient walls. Dancing fluorescent bulbs dangle from its ceiling, wind-generating fans are fastened to its walls, and ancient tiles cover the floor.

Many notices are taped on its walls: one for *Sefiras ha'Omer*, another announcing *zeman Kriyas Shema* and *tefillah*, and one reminding worshippers that it's forbidden to talk in shul. The numerous signs define the worshippers' *tefillah* obligations and admonish them to respect the sanctity of the shul.

On the longest winter Motza'ei Shabbosim and the shortest summer ones, whether the nights are as hot as the oven of Achnai or as cold as the North Pole, the Chassidim gather in Batei Rand to escort the Queen with a modest meal. They make a *berachah* on challah from Shabbos, take a few bites of herring with onions and peppers, and finish the leftovers that each Chassid brings from his house. Together they sing the Motza'ei Shabbos *zemiros* and listen to an elder who tells a tale of tzaddikim as per the *minhag* of Chassidim on Motza'ei Shabbos.

Wine awaits them on the wide windowsill so they can be "*mezamen al hakos*"; they then go home to begin a week of pure *avodas Hashem*, following the same traditions that have been followed in Batei Rand since its establishment.

"

Every evening, a mysterious *chavrusa* would come to learn Torah with him, next to his sewing machine. As they learned, passersby claimed to have seen *seraphim* flying between the Singer and Bernina sewing machines, and *malachim* hovering between his foot pedal and the needle.

("The Mysterious Tailor," page 84)

Chapter Two
Anshei Yerushalayim

אשר נתן לשכוי בינה

"Who Gave to the Rooster Understanding"

It is said that there is not one act of kindness that Reb Leizer Shafer didn't do nor was there a poor person within his *dalet amos* who he didn't try to help.

It is also said that nothing compares to the sight of Reb Leizer standing near the Batei Wittenberg shul holding a colorful, crowned chicken in honor of the Shabbos Queen. On snowy days, Reb Leizer cleared the alleys leading to the shul, ensuring that the residents would be able to walk safely without slipping or breaking a limb, *chas v'shalom*.

Reb Leizer had a motor vehicle — a *"kenack beizik"* — a noisy bike, also known as a moped. He used his moped for *chesed* and gave people rides. He used to take a dear friend, one of the greatest *ovdei Hashem* in Yerushalayim, to purify himself in the natural spring on the slopes of Motza, on the outskirts of Yerushalayim. They used to ride on the moped, helmets on their heads per the commandment of *"venishmartem."* Ultimately, this friend became a great Rebbe with thousands of Chassidim streaming to his doorstep.

Reb Leizer's custom of crossing under the curved arches of Batei Wittenberg on Erev Shabbos with a rooster on his shoulder was entertainment for the children of Yerushalayim. They walked behind him, chattering about the marvels of the crowned bird and the magic of the extraordinary man who carried it *l'kavod Shabbos*. The deep-rooted Yerushalayim purity reigned when Reb Leizer would bring the rooster to the slaughterhouse, so that it could finish its *tikkun* and be served to the Yerushalmi dignitaries on Friday night.

הַחִיוּךְ שֶׁל רֶב אַבִּי׳שׁ
Reb Abish's Smile

Every wrinkle and crease on Rav Abish Eizen's face testifies to each of his life's experiences. Yet there is nobody else in Yerushalayim who, with his *simchas hachaim*, merits to bring joy and happiness to others like Reb Abish.

Reb Abish attends every *bris milah* and *kiddush*, every bar mitzvah and wedding. His mazel tov wishes are so heartfelt that the *ba'al simchah* thinks, *Although this is not Reb Abish's simchah, he is ten times happier than I.*

Nobody should ever know misfortune, but when tragedy occurs in Givat Shaul, where he lives, Reb Abish is present to join in the family's pain as if he himself suffered misfortune.

Although Reb Abish's face is creased with age, his eyes sparkle with a glint of good-humored mischievousness. Joy is always visible on his face, but when he attends a *levayah* or *shivah*, he wraps himself in sadness. He is in full control of his moods, like a potter forming his wares. Just as he can increase his joviality or do something silly in order to pull someone out of depression, he can diminish his cheerfulness in order to empathize with a mourning family.

Reb Abish isn't a man who discriminates. His neighborhood is inhabited by Perushim and Chassidim, Yerushalmis and those from Bnei Brak, *kanaim* and Agudah members. He doesn't differentiate between communities and *hashkafos*.

Neighbors testify that when someone from Givat Shaul stops Reb Abish to inform him that he was blessed with a new baby, Reb Abish takes the father's hands and dances with him in the street. The blaring horns and angry drivers don't bother him; now it's time to rejoice with a fellow Jew who was blessed with *zera shel kayama*.

Reb Abish's pockets are filled with taffies. Not only children enjoy them, but at times he has been known to dole them out to adults who are already proud grandparents. Reb Abish visits the Herzog Hospital every day, and with his simple, captivating charm, he's able to bring a smile to the faces of the hospitalized patients.

כל הנשמה תהלל
Let All Souls Praise

There was one special individual in the "Shtetlach" whose name was Rav Yitzchak Nosson Kuperstock, a person who illuminated his environment and a *gaon* who constantly learned Torah. His eyes reflected a profound, penetrating look and his essence spoke of simple, quiet *yiras haromemus*.

Many were saved by his heartfelt prayers, uttered with purity, concentration, great deliberation, and a keen focus that was safeguarded for Hashem. It's been said that even as a young thirty-year-old *avreich*, he was given names for prayer by his Rebbe, the Gaon of Tschebin.

On Fridays, Rav Yitzchak Nosson would awaken before sunrise and daven *k'vasikin* in Batei Broide, then travel to Beis Lechem and recite the entire *Sefer Tehillim* by *Kever Rachel*.

This weekly event was six hours long. Six hours of pleading to Hashem for the good of the community as well as for individuals. Each and every word was uttered carefully, and with great deliberation. Nothing else pressured him. The tears that fell dampened the pages and created a screen between his pure eyes and the rest of the world.

During the Second Intifada, when it was dangerous to travel to Beis Lechem, he would say the entire *Tehillim* at the entrance to his house, right where he lit the Chanukah menorah.

גאון בצידי דרכים

On the Side of the Road

The *gaonim* of Yerushalayim are very different from *gaonim* in the rest of the world. Usually, a Torah scholar is extolled and praised, seated on the *mizrach*, and greeted with a boisterous rendition of *"Yamim al yemei melech tosif."*

But in Yerushalayim, Torah giants walk on the sides of the road, surreptitiously slipping into their hideaways and evading publicity. Rav Chaim Brim *zt"l*, a confidante of the Chazon Ish, was this type of Torah luminary. He was always rushing on his way to daven and learn, with the pure *yiras Shamayim*, majestic Chassidus, extra *perishus*, and incredible genius that encompassed his daily activities. As a child, I merited to receive his gracious warmth, encouraging words, and a *sefer* that he gifted to me at my bar mitzvah celebration.

He was a genius and a leader of his generation, but since he lived in Yerushalayim and absorbed its personality and character traits, he was most comfortable in his private corner, breathing the holy letters of the Torah twenty-four hours a day.

What of *"Yamim al yemei melech tosif"*? The *Pamalya shel Maalah* will greet him with this song when he arrives in Gan Eden, where the words of Chazal, *"Man malchi? Rabanan"* reign true.

החנות של הויזמן
Hausman's Store

Few can describe the merchandise sold in the store of Rav Aharon Hausman, an elderly Karliner Chassid. On the counter are old *sefarim*, ancient *tashmishei kedushah*, dangling strands of tzitzis and yellowed objects that make his store seem like a museum on the history of Meah Shearim.

Truthfully, it's hard to know how much merchandise Rav Aharon actually sold and how much money he had in his register — were he to use one in his store. What you did acquire in his store were quality *"da'as z'keinim"* in the form of stories and anecdotes about the previous righteous generations. Rav Aharon did not disappoint. He was the source for Chassidish stories, especially those that described the greatness of the Karliner Rebbe and his elder Chassidim in Teveriah and Yerushalayim.

The door of his store was covered with layers of Yerushalmi *pashkevils* that were planted by neighborhood *kanaim*: those who mourn the "forty years of rebellion against *malchus Shamayim*" (the age of Israel back then) and a plethora of notices protesting transgressions that cause Eretz Yisrael to tremble.

When it was time to close up, Rav Aharon seemed bent over by the weight of the notices hanging on his door, but he never complained. At most, he reminded himself of stories he heard from elder Chassidim between the two world wars, and thus encouraged himself. At the end of his life, he gathered all of these memories into a *sefer* entitled *Parach Mateh Aharon*. There are those who say this was the real item sold in his store — the true transmission of the past.

קירות מדברים

Talking Walls

The *pashkevils* in Meah Shearim are an institution in their own right. Every topic is discussed on the neighborhood's walls: cancelled *kashrus* certification, protests, fundraising appeals, and how to check onions for bugs.

The sacred goal of identifying spiritual stumbling blocks and admonishing others about them has led to a flourishing *pashkevil* industry. For the Yerushalmis who are disconnected from all media sources, the street signs are their only source of information and an inseparable part of daily life.

So eager are they to find out what is written on these notices that they try to take a peek at them while they're still in the *pashkevil*-paster's bike, before they're hung on the walls. This picture was taken in the Meah Shearim *shuk*, at the entrance to the building used by the Neturei Karta, a community known for its own booming *pashkevil* industry.

גלויה
מה'גוׇלדֶענֶע
מֶעדִינֶע'

Postcard from the "Goldeneh Medinah"

Two things connect the Jews of Meah Shearim to those in Williamsburg: the money for tzedakah and the newspapers sent from far-off Brooklyn to Yerushalayim.

The Jews of Meah Shearim, who often don't have a penny to their names, read the Yiddish newspapers that are imported from Williamsburg and Monroe: *Der Yid* of the *"Zaloynim"* (the Chassidim of Admor Yekusiel Yehudah of Satmar) and *Der Blatt* of the *"Aroynim"* (Chassidim of Admor Aharon of Satmar). These newspapers are read in addition to the eternal *Ha'eidah*, upon whose administration Rav Yaakov Roth, the legendary store owner, serves as a member.

These are the sole newspapers in existence; no others can be found here. If one wants to read other *chareidi* newspapers, he has to leave this sheltered neighborhood and venture out to the *"pitzuchim"* stores on Malchei Yisrael Street.

נפתלי סנדלר קדוש

Naftali the Holy Shoemaker

Whoever enters Reb Naftali's store leaves with much more than repaired shoes: Reb Naftali arms his customers with a thought on the weekly *parashah* or a Yerushalmi story about the famous figures of years past.

A *chosson* buying shoes for his wedding hears a *peshat* on the famous saying *"invei hagefen b'invei hagefen"* and a bar mitzvah boy leaves the workshop with not only strong shoes on his feet, but a fascinating story about a *Gadol* as well.

The following is a classic story that Reb Naftali told me during one of my visits to his workshop:

"When I was a young bar mitzvah boy, I was walking past the Shtieblach on my way to *cheder* when I heard someone calling, '*A tzenter, Mincheh! A tzenter, Mincheh!*' I went into the Shtieblach and saw six people sitting there — but not just any people — five of them were *Gedolei HaDor*: Rebbe Mordechai of Slonim, Rebbe Shlomo of Zhvill, Rav Gershon Lapidus, Rav Elkanah Weisenstern, and Rav Shimon Aharon Polansky of Teplik. They were all *gaonim* and *mekubalim*, saintly, holy people, and were waiting for a minyan for Minchah! And I, the young bar mitzvah boy, helped them complete their minyan!"

"A nice story, you hear — huh?" Reb Naftali Bornstein asked after telling over the story. I personally saw people enter his workshop with no intention other than to be enveloped by the wisdom and benevolence of Reb Naftali, a survivor of the Jordanian captivity, who *leins* every Shabbos, and who sings out "*Mimkomcha*" with gusto.

ילדי מחניים

The Children of "Machanayim"

This is a scene that the deceased Henryk Hechtkopf would have loved to illustrate.

The Ein Yaakov *sefarim* store, located across from the Meah Shearim *shtieblach*, was owned by Reb Yankel Roth, a member of the *hanhalah* of the Eidah HaChareidis, a Jew with a flowing beard, a brow that radiates sincerity, and a figure that exudes *yir'as Shamayim*.

Someone invited to a bar mitzvah can't arrive at the event without first stopping in Reb Yankel Roth's store to buy a simple edition of the *Mesillas Yesharim* or a different *sefer* that costs fifteen shekels or less.

Sefer in hand, he proceeds to the event hall, usually an upgraded storage room. There he tastes a piece of kugel with a pickle at its side, the only refreshments served at a Yerushalmi bar mitzvah.

The children of Meah Shearim don't have money to buy books. That's why they stand at the entrance of the store and read the soft-covered *Machanayim* booklets, illustrated by the aforementioned Henryk Hechtkopf. These books engrain *emunas chachamim* and *yir'as Shamayim* in the hearts of young readers.

Because the children read continuously at the entrance of the store, passersby can easily mistake the *sefarim* store for a neighborhood library. About once an hour, the storeowner angrily chases the children away in order to clear the entrance for people to come in and buy a *Mesillas Yesharim* on their way to a bar mitzvah.

החייט המסתורי

The Mysterious Tailor

Some say that the old Sephardi tailor at the entrance to Meah Shearim Street was one of the thirty-six hidden tzaddikim, and that if he wasn't one of the thirty-six, he was at least the thirty-seventh. Everybody agrees that he served Hashem with needle and thread like the tailors of long ago; his lips murmured words of Torah whenever he had a free moment.

He actually had many free moments, since Yerushalmi women are quite adept with thimble and needle and don't spend money on tailoring services.

The tailor was a solitary Sephardi in a *shuk* that was primarily Ashkenazi. He sat on the main road of Meah Shearim and accepted clothing from Yerushalmi women who, despite it all, couldn't manage to sew on their own. There were always faded suits hanging next to him, waiting to be mended, and old pairs of pants waiting to be patched.

Every evening, a mysterious *chavrusa* would come to learn Torah with him, next to his sewing machine. As they learned, passersby claimed to have seen *seraphim* flying between the Singer and Bernina sewing machines and *malachim* hovering between his foot pedal and the needle.

בחנות של רֶב פַיבַלֶ'ה
In Reb Feivele's Store

The storekeepers in Meah Shearim are cut from a different cloth than storekeepers in the rest of the world. They're never in a hurry, and their efforts to earn a living don't dull their sensitivities or confuse their priorities.

Stores in Meah Shearim don't have cash registers, only scales. They don't even have price tags — just a metal board where the storekeeper marks the price of each product with chalk.

Every day the storekeeper brings new produce from the Machaneh Yehudah *shuk* or similar marketplaces, after which a stern-looking *mashgiach* from the "Eidah" comes to *ma'aser* the fruits and vegetables.

The legendary Reb Feivel Wallerstein was one such storekeeper. His store at the entrance to the *shuk* carried some vegetables that added a few shekels to his pocket. But for someone like Reb Feivel, a survivor of the Nazi inferno, the hardships of earning a living were of no more concern than the worthless peels of garlic that he hung at the entrance to his store — just as Meah Shearim storekeepers and housekeepers have always done for reasons known only to them.

He never forgot the atrocities of the Holocaust and his spirit was pained by all that the Nazi animals did to his nation and family. His store wasn't always full of vegetables or customers, but he was always there at his post, serving as a heroic figure, a Jew who held onto his faith despite the terrible poison he imbibed. Reb Feivel's store is flanked by another one, run by an elderly Sephardi Jew from Meah Shearim named Peretz. But in Reb Feivel's world there is no rivalry; there is only Hakadosh Baruch Hu.

Mischievous children sometimes made fun of him, but Reb Feivel endured many crises and insisted on surviving. He produced generations of descendants who follow the *mesorah* the Nazis tried so hard to obliterate, thereby defeating them each and every day.

Reb Feivel endured, persevered, and remained faithful — the eternal victor!

מה לך נרדם
What Are You Doing Sleeping?

Hame'orer Yesheinim — that is how everybody referred to Reb El'e Weinberger, a *talmid* of Reb Aharele of Shomrei Emunim. Day and night, he sat in his room across from the Meah Shearim *shtieblach* and studied his *sefarim* and manuscripts. A large sign hanging in the store that sold nothing announced that this was the *"Cheder Hame'orerim,"* named for the inspiring *kuntressim* that he published from time to time.

Rav Eliyahu was a very quiet person; many were not familiar with his words of inspiration, but everyone was impressed by his intensity and insightfulness. He sat and served his Creator from morning until night in his little store. A heater warmed him during the rains and a fan cooled him during the heat. There was always a sign announcing a "distribution of *sefarim* to yeshivos and *kollelim*." Which *sefarim*? What yeshivos and *kollelim*? We'll never know exactly. It's sufficient to get a glimpse of this extraordinary person, a vestige of the *"dor de'ah,"* to garner some concept of what true *avodas Hashem* looks like.

His son, *yibadel l'chaim*, sat just a few stores away, making *batim* for tefillin. Since his "*batim*" store was so close to the *"Cheder Hame'orerim,"* the *"batim-macher"* took a break every few minutes to peek in and see how his father was doing. Truth be told, there was no greater embodiment of *kibud av va'em* in the whole world.

Nowadays, since Rav Eliyahu the *"me'orer"* is no longer with us, *avreichim* looking to earn an honest living use the room to sell *arba minim*, while the spirit of Rav Eliyahu hovers above them.

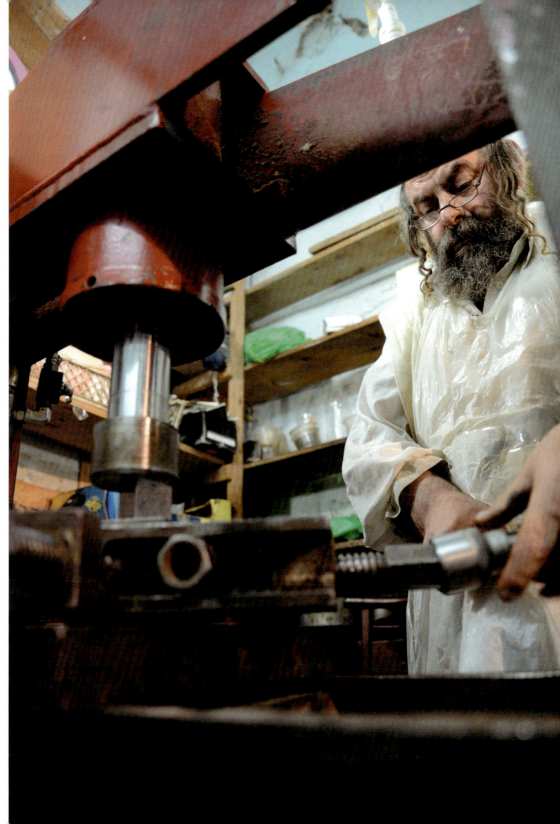

והחי יתן אל ליבו

THE LIVING SHOULD TAKE IT TO HEART

When a person's life comes to an end, the loudspeaker goes around the streets of Meah Shearim announcing that the *levayah* of so-and-so will leave from this-and-this place at a certain time to Har HaZeisim or Har HaMenuchos. The people of Meah Shearim are meticulous about paying their respects to the deceased by escorting them on foot until their final resting place. Those who are *mehader* in this mitzvah carry the *aron* with their own hands and thereby physically fulfill the mitzvah of *chesed shel emes*.

This is the way of the world, and this is how it's done in the neighborhood that is blessed with elderly people. These people have survived twelve generations and are familiar with death entering through the window, when the time has come for a neighbor to pack the bag of his life and the bundle of his soul. When the deceased is a learned person who spent most of his life in Torah and good deeds, nobody feels bad. Instead, they are jealous of he who merits to ascend to the world of only good and enjoy all that awaits tzaddikim.

In this picture, you can see the diverse residents of Meah Shearim waiting to escort a friend to his eternal home. They take advantage of the time to talk about the history and virtues of the man whose *neshamah* is making its way to the *ginzei Olamim*, until such time that death is wiped out forever and those resting in the dust will awaken and rejoice at the end of days.

סוף כל האדם

The End of Every Man

A Yerushalmi *levayah* that takes place under heavy rain is different than a *levayah* in the sun, but the elders of Yerushalayim aren't deterred by pelting rain and don't let that stop them from paying their respects to one who deserves it.

In the picture on the facing page, masses of Yerushalmis are seen escorting Rav Yisrael Yaakov Fisher, *Gaavad* of the Badatz and legendary *dayan*, whose sharp genius blended with a unique soft, fatherly warmth.

In Yerushalayim, many *levayah*s are held at night, due to the ancient stringency not to leave a *niftar* unburied overnight. In the above picture, the *Gedolim* and *talmidei chachamim* of the Yishuv stand at the entrance of the Chassidish shul in Batei Ungarin. They are escorting Rav Leibish Deutsch, who spent his whole life delving into Torah and collapsed while walking to give a *shiur* in the Chabad Shul in Meah Shearim.

In Yerushalayim, *mechitzos* are unnecessary at *levayahs*. A path forms automatically, with the men on one side and the women on the other, while together they mourn the *shufra d'karta d'bali be'ara*.

בגנזי מרומים

IN THE HEAVENLY REALM

Har HaZeisim is where the members of the Yishuv Hayashan want to be buried. Their fathers are buried there; some with graves marked with stone *matzeivah*s and others that have been ploughed and obliterated over time by the Yishmaelites.

At all hours of the day there are Yerushalmis climbing the mountain, lighting olive oil flames near the graves of *Gedolei Olam*, and offering up pure, untarnished prayers.

In this picture, Rav Yossel Sheinberger *zt"l* is seen visiting the grave of Rabbeinu Moshe Yehoshua Leib Diskin *zy"a*, Rav of Yerushalayim, on his *yahrtzeit*. Rav Yossel was the secretary of the Eidah HaChareidis and clung to the holy fire of the Maharil Diskin. Therefore, on the *yahrtzeit* of the Maharil, Rav Sheinberger climbed the mountain to pour out his heartfelt *tefillah*.

Rav Yossel climbed, supported by his grandchildren: on his left, one grandson, and on his right, another grandson, Rav Meir Sirota *zt"l*, a sensitive *avreich* who, tragically, was *niftar* a short time later. Together they stood at the *kever* of the Maharil and bonded with mysterious, holy worlds.

At the same time, three Yerushalmi *mekubalim* stood in a different section of the mountain and davened at the tomb of Rabbeinu Chaim ibn Attar *zy"a*, the Ohr Hachaim Hakadosh, admired and revered by the Ashkenazi residents of Yerushalayim who learn his Torah teachings at all times. May we be protected by their merit.

> It is said that if this old-fashioned wooden table would be able to speak like, *l'havdil*, Bila'am's donkey, Yerushalayim would have a hard time internalizing all that it absorbed over the course of a hundred years of continuous Torah and Chassidus. The table is saturated with holy words, moving testimony of the tens of thousands of magnificent moments that penetrated it. This table embodies mountains of tears and *avodas halev*; the *gabbaim* wouldn't dare replace it.

("The Yoke of Heavenly Sovereignty," page 102)

Chapter Three
Batei Midrashos

עול מלכות שמים
The Yoke of Heavenly Sovereignty

If not for the countless rusty nails banged into the antiquated, heavy wooden table that adorns the corner of the Chabad Shul, the table would have long ago turned into flames. It would have been snatched by the adrenalin-blessed children of Meah Shearim collecting wood for their Lag Ba'Omer fire. It is said that if this old-fashioned wooden table would be able to speak like, *l'havdil*, Bila'am's donkey, Yerushalayim would have a hard time internalizing all that it absorbed over the course of a hundred years of continuous Torah and Chassidus. The table is saturated with holy words, moving testimony of the tens of thousands of

magnificent moments that penetrated it. This table embodies mountains of tears and *avodas halev*; the *gabbaim* wouldn't dare replace it. Since 1909, Chassidim have sat around it and proudly served their Creator.

Rav Moshe Weber *zt"l*, who nurtured me, was one such tzaddik. He sat here throughout his life, his heart softened with Torah, *tefillah*, and *kiruv rechokim*. His *avodah* never ceased; not when he was strong nor when he was weak and sick.

The giant glass holders filled to the rim with pure olive oil could burn for long days like the western flame of the Menorah, testimony to the *chassidei emes* who cleave to their *avodah*. Just as those flames burn, the flame within their own hearts always burns.

The deer illustrated in the domed ceiling diverts his gaze from his neighbors — the lion, leopard, and eagle — and smiles with satisfaction: over here Chassidus lives and grows stronger, continuing in the ways of old.

טעם זקנים

A Taste of the Wise

The *talmidei chachamim* of Yerushalayim don't seek out honor; they are the embodiment of simplicity and goodheartedness.

Although their daily schedule revolves around learning and teaching Torah, they don't wear *"frocks"* or *"hamburgs."* They dress in simple clothing, a *"chalat"* or striped coat and a wide-brimmed hat, with a shining-white knitted yarmulke underneath it.

This is Rav Leibish Deutsch *zt"l*. Every Erev Sukkos, masses of people would flow to his house so that he could check their

esrogim with his special magnifying glass along with his extensive knowledge of *hilchos arba minim* and all halachos in the *Shulchan Aruch*.

Rav Leibish wore a light-green caftan and white pants — just like the Yerushalmis wore a hundred years ago. Every evening, he gave a Mishnayos *shiur* in the Chabad Shul on Ba'al HaTanya Street, *l'iluy nishmas* the departed.

Rav Leibish Herzl *zt"l* was Rav Leibish Deutsch's *chavrusa*. These two "lions" had been learning Mishnayos together when Yehudah, who davened in the Sephardi Shul, asked them to teach him Torah. They answered him graciously and set a time for a *shiur*.

One time, Rav Leibish Deutsch arrived at the shul, stuck his key in the lock, but couldn't turn it. He called his son, known to be an expert locksmith, and pleaded with him to come quickly, in order to save him from *bittul Torah*.

While waiting for R' Uri the locksmith, Reb Leibish collapsed. The man whose entire life was filled with teaching Mishnayos passed away at his post, and the tens of thousands of Mishnayos that he learned and taught ascended along with him.

חבוקה ודבוקה בך

With All Your Heart

Rav Mordechai Leib Zukerman was a leader of Torah and *mussar*. Starting from the day he was born in the village of Ladvoda on the 5 Adar 1912 until he passed away on Shabbos Kodesh *Parashas Vayera*, 20 MarCheshvan 2003, Torah and *perishus* were his entire life. You would leave him in the morning in the corner of the shul in Givat Shaul leaning over his Gemara, and find him in the same position that evening.

He was one of the last *talmidim* of the Chofetz Chaim. He learned in the Radin Yeshivah for two and a half years while Rabbeinu Yisrael Meir HaKohen was still alive. Rav Mordechai Leib merited to hear the Chofetz Chaim's *shmuessen* every Friday night between *Lechu Neranenah* and *Bameh Madlikin*, and during the shadowy darkness after Shalosh Seudos.

When an artist approached him with a picture he had sketched of his great Rebbe, Rav Mordechai Lcib said, "I don't need a picture of the Chofetz Chaim because his image stands before my eyes throughout my life. Whatever I do, I think to myself: What would Mori v'Rabi say about this?"

And what did Rav Mordechai Leib do? He learned Torah with all his heart.

המקובלים של 'אנשי מעמד'
The Mekubalim of "Anshei Ma'amad"

The Anshei Ma'amad Beis Midrash, where the elder *mekubalim* of Meah Shearim sit and delve into the mystical *sefarim* — forbidden to those who haven't yet reached the age of *binah* — makes a striking image of picturesque beauty in ancient times.

The Chassid Rav Daniel Frisch *zt"l* was a prominent *mekubal*. His commentary, *Masok Midvash*, fulfills its title; it's as sweet as honey. It explains the *Zohar* and the Idras according to the Ramak and Rabbeinu Chaim Vital, and opens a window into Kabbalah. This commentary was developed during the *shiur* that he gave in Anshei Ma'amad, surrounded by Yerushalami elders and *mekubalim* from all factions — *perushim*, Toldos Aharon Chassidim, and any type of Chassidim that wanted to learn the wisdom of truth. Rav Daniel Frisch invited *chassanim* into his home, supplied them with *sefarim* to help enrich their homes with *kedushah* and *perishus*, taught them the essence of *yiras Hashem*, and engraved unforgettable impressions upon their hearts.

אנשים של 'שויתי'
The People of "Shivisi"

Rav Anschel Bruin *zt"l* was a Yerushalami *gadol* and a *sofer stam*. His study, where he slept, was decorated with parchment that he had inscribed in his own hand: *Shivisi Hashem l'negdi samid*, with the *Shem Hameforash*.

At the time the photographer asked to take a picture of him writing, he was old, weak, and frail, and bent over his Gemara. "I'm sick, and I don't write anymore," he said with the serene composure of a true Yerushalmi. With this *middah*, one can speak of happy occasions as well as disturbing troubles while maintaining the same pure facial expression. Complaints or grievances are never voiced.

"The street is full of dirt," he whispered to the photographer. When he said the words *"di gass"* — the street — his eyes reflected scorn and denigration. There he sat, in his room, living in a magical world of hs own, a world of friendship and incredible *deveikus*.

This picture was taken in Anshei Ma'amad, where Rav Anschel sat every day. He is being *mispalpel* (a *"kutzmeh"* hat on his head) with Rav Abish Tzeinvirt *shlita*, a prominent *mekubal*, along with a young *avreich*.

The other picture depicts Rav Dovid Schlensiger, a spiritual giant of Yerushalayim, who lives in a small house in Batei Ungarin, next door to Mori V'Rabi Rav Moshe Weber *zt"l*. He stands on the porch next to the Perushim Shul in Batei Ungarin, which over the years has been converted into a library.

החייל הזקן בעולם

The Oldest Soldier in the World

Rav Velvel Eisenbach zt"l's one hundred and two years were filled with *limud* and *tefillah* — and *tefillah* and *limud*. I used to refer to him as "the oldest soldier in the world" when I'd see him in the morning, walking quickly to the *mikveh*. Even though he circulated among us in the twentieth and twenty-first century, he didn't really belong here: he was a page torn out of an ancient Vilna *Shas*.

His day began at two o'clock every morning in the Toldos Aharon *mikveh* next to his house, in Batei Ungarin. He then recited the entire *Sefer Tehillim* before boarding the bus to the Kosel, where he davened *vasikin*. The rest of his day would then be divided between dozens of *batei midrashim* and *kollels*, where he was just a "regular" *avreich*. He would start in "Anshei Ma'amad" and finish at the *kabbalah shiur* given by Rav Moshe Weber zt"l on the *Sha'ar Hakavanos* to a group of *yechidei segulah* who were conversant in the mystical aspects of Torah.

One Rosh Hashanah, as we were walking back from davening, we heard the news of Rav Velvel's death at the age of 102. Despite his age, the news was shocking, as if a young man had died suddenly of a heart attack, because Reb Velvel *had* been a young *avreich* his entire life.

When he passed away, he left behind more than one thousand two hundred descendants. He had progeny in all factions of *chareidi* Jewry, including some in Gur (Rav Chanina Schiff was his son-in-law), Belz, the yeshivah world, Toldos Aharon, and Neturei Karta.

During *bein hasedarim* in Anshei Ma'amad, Rav Velvel fought his fatigue by standing next to an open window. He was short with a thin body, white beard, and furrowed brow, but he thought only about one thing: Torah.

He told us, the students of "Shomrei HaChomos," during the daily tests he gave us in the narrow room at the end of the hallway, "*Toireh is di beste sechoirah*" — Torah is the best merchandise in the world.

Here, Rav Anschel Bruin sits near to him, also learning with *dveikus*. Between the two, they have lived close to two hundred years and have more than two thousand descendants. Their vitality is rooted in the same source; it is the reason for their lucidity and the secret of their lengthy days: *Toireh is di beste sechoirah*.

יהודים, נקמה
Jewish Revenge

What are the wellsprings from which two noble Jews of Meah Shearim draw their strength, the strength of character to forge on after their family members were burnt at the stake during the terrible days of the Holocaust and to move to Eretz Yisrael without anything at all? If you want to know, find these two simple Yerushalmi working men after a day of holy work making *batim for tefillin* by taking a step into the side shul where these Hungarian immigrants sit and place all that they've endured behind them.

There they sit with purity of heart, Rav Schwartz and Rav Kaufman, on the long, desolate nights of Teves and the sweltering nights of Tammuz, delving into the *sugya* and hewing golden treasures from it.

They learn with unsullied souls, with faces shining like the sun and using friendly hand gestures. No worries trouble them as they sit and learn Torah with vitality, dedication, and unparalleled purity of heart. This is the living well from which these two, who drank the cup of sorrow in their youth, now join together every evening to take their eternal revenge against the Nazi enemy.

כתלי בית המדרש

The Walls of the Beis Midrash

An infinite timbre of antiquity rests between the walls of the Yeshuos Yaakov Shul, one of the oldest shuls in Meah Shearim. This shul is located under the floor of the Tiferes Bachurim Beis Midrash, where Rabbeinu Yosef Shalom Elyashiv *zt"l* gave his *shiur* for close to eighty years.

The walls, floor, and benches of Yeshuos Yaakov are testimony to the spiritual giants who walked here and sanctified it with holiness. One such giant was Rav Chaim Brim *zy"a*, who lived nearby. On Shabbos morning, he davened in this shul. He would purify himself before his Creator by davening before the *amud* for Musaf with tremendous *yiras Shamayim*.

Rav Asher Lederman *zt"l* had a steady schedule that continued throughout the course of the day. He would daven until *chatzos* and then seat himself on a bench in Yeshuos Yaakov to learn Torah. Behind him danced the eternal flames that were lit in honor of the deceased; while he sat there, his own *ner neshamah* ascended and joined the *Heichalos shel Maalah*.

אמריקה נוסח ירושלים

America: The Yerushalmi Version

There's a small room in Meah Shearim that's called the "Amerikaner Shul." You may search its nooks and crannies, but you won't find any stars and stripes. So why is it called the American Shul? Because over a hundred years ago, the donors who helped found the shul were from America. Generally, North America has always kindled the imagination of the Yishuv

Hayashan because of the rumor that gold coins roll freely on its streets. America is *"De Goldeneh Medinah"* — the Land of Gold. If donors from the Golden Land sent money to build a *beis midrash*, that's sufficient justification for giving it a name that could have easily been mistaken for a US embassy.

Other than its name, the shul is devoid of any other American symbols. Elderly laborers begin their day here with Shacharis at *vasikin*, followed by a *halachah shiur*. They also conclude their day here with Minchah and Maariv, with a *shiur* in between on Ein Yaakov and Daf Yomi, given by HaRav Frankel *zt"l*, a member of the Badatz. In the picture above, an old *Yid* toils over his Gemara, his fingers creased and nails yellowed; nothing in this world compares to the profound *peirush* of the Ran on *Perek Arba'ah Nedarim*.

American or not — there is nothing sweeter in the world than the sight of these elderly *ba'alei batim* sitting in the twilight, overcoming their fatigue and learning Torah, connecting to the well from which the Jewish Nation draws its eternity.

The Depths of Halachah

There is one place in Yerushalayim that unites Torah sages from all factions of *chareidi* Jewry.

One sage is Yerushalmi through and through. His friend's very essence is Litvish. A third sage's ten *"kochos"* are all Chabad and a fourth is a Gerer Chassid with Polish *charifus*. Every Friday, these four meet for an unparalleled learning *seder*.

What's the connection between a Yerushalmi, a Litvishe, a Gerer Chassid, and a Chabad Chassid? There's a good answer to that question: they all share one Torah. The Torah is one. It is shared by all who study it, especially the *talmidei chachamim* and *anshei yirah* in *Yerushalayim shel Maalah*.

They gather together in the picturesque shul in Batei Wittenberg, open volumes of the *Shulchan Aruch* and simmer in the heat of Torah. Like a boiling pot whose steam penetrates the air around it, the heat of their Torah penetrates the thick walls of the shul that's as old as the Yishuv Hayashan.

The Litvak reads the *halachah* as it's written in the source. The Gerer poses a serious question. The Yerushalmi suggests an answer and the Chabadnik refutes it. The four begin a give-and-take; they wrangle and clarify and open and close *sefarim* until the *sugya* is illuminated and as clear as it was when given at Sinai.

Immense satisfaction reigns and the pleasures of the world are dwarfed by the bliss that exists in Batei Wittenberg when the Chabad Chassid, the Yerushalmi, Litvak, and Gerer Chassid join together to draw water from the eternal wellspring.

הוֹי, כֹּל צָמֵא

Thirsty for Torah

The walls of the "second room" in the Hungarisher Shul — the shul in Batei Ungarin — are permeated with immeasurable Torah. The windows are rickety, the walls are peeling, and the shelves are worn from old age, yet a divine sweetness presides in the long, narrow, rectangular room where the people of Batei Ungarin have sat and learned Torah for more than one hundred years.

A fire of *ahavas HaTorah* burns in Mishkenot Haroim as well, the "Marmishe Shul," located in the center of Meah Shearim Street, but named for the village of Maramures, Romania. This shul was led by Rav Binyamin Rabinowitz *zt"l*; its holy *kehillah* keeps its distance from the folly of this world. On the facing page is Rav Yehudah Leib Frank *zt"l*, his face radiant with the light of Torah. Despite his busy schedule, he makes sure to learn, taking time off from being an experienced *mohel*, from being *mekarev gerei tzedek*, and from distributing worn clothes to the poor of Yerushalayim — for which he earned the honorific *"Frank fun di shmattes."*

חזקת בעלי הבתים
A Tradition of Torah

Day and night, the sound of Torah emanates from the Ohel Rachel Shul, the crowning glory of the picturesque Knesses Yisrael neighborhood in the "Shtetlach." The shul is neither big nor grand in its physical measurements, but its spiritual greatness is indescribable. Old wooden bookcases, with even older *sefarim*, cover its walls. The neighborhood elders pull out large, antiquated Gemaras from its shelves and, through them, bond to Hashem's Torah.

The Yerushalmi tzaddik, Rav Aryeh Levin *zt"l*, gave a daily Gemara *shiur* in this shul. After his death, his son Rav Refael *zt"l* assumed his father's position and gave the *shiur* in his stead.

When Rav Refael passed away, his son, *yibadel l'chaim aruchim*, took over his father's and grandfather's position and till this day gives the family *shiur* to a rare collection of Jews. The *shiur* participants embody "*kibbutz galuyos*": *kipot serugot* and black hats, Israeli-born and Russian immigrants. Above all, next to the sign stating "Don't talk in shul!" hovers the spirit of the Yerushalmi tzaddik, smiling down on those learning and saying, "Lucky are you who toil in Torah."

או חברותא או מיתותא

A Chavrusa More Precious than Life

On Simchas Torah, we were allowed a glimpse into the hidden personalities of the *gaonim* Rav Shimon Jakobovitz and Rav Aharon Mordechai Zilberstrum. The rest of the year, they remained quiet, hiding the secrets of their hearts. But Simchas Torah was different.

Seven days a week, a thermos of tea rested on the table of the Chabad Shul in the Meah Shearim *shuk*. Around the table sat Rav Shimon and Rav Aharon Mordechai, Chassidim and *gaonim* who were "*kanah chachmah*" their whole lives, yet their only desire was to continue and ascend even higher in their *avodas*

Hashem. They discussed Torah, clapping their hands with excitement, took sip after sip of the tea, and demanded more and more of themselves as if they were still young Chassidim.

For decades, day after day, they learned together, finishing the entire *Shas* and the *Mishneh Torah* of the Rambam, Rabbeinu Moshe ben Maimon, annually. Here they sat for long hours, learning Torah and completely detached from this world.

On Motza'ei Shabbos *Parashas Balak* 2012, the Meah Shearim *shuk* became black from the masses of people who came to be *melaveh* the *aron* of Rav Aharon Mordechai Zilberstrum. The crowds of humanity that blocked the entrances to the *shuk* were in deep pain over the loss of the unsullied, pure *neshamah* that passed on after eighty-nine years of glory. Rav Shimon Jakobovitz was one of those who accompanied his dear friend, feeling as though half of his *neshamah* had just been uprooted.

Just a few months later, after eighty years of uninterrupted Torah study, Rav Shimon too was taken to the *Mesivta D'rakiah*.

שבעתיים כאור החמה
A Blazing Sun

A spiritual giant lived in the "Shtetlach," extraordinary in his genius, wondrous in his greatness: Rav Zundel Kroizer *zt"l*. He educated many *talmidim*, and with great humility conveyed *ahavas haTorah*, demanding neither honor nor respect.

For nearly his entire life he lived in Batei Broide. His genius was a byword, his *hasmadah* a wonder. But even so, he was kind and compassionate. He assisted the needy, established a *gemach* for those with limited resources, and sold eggs and other food products at less than cost price to benefit *talmidei chachamim* who could not afford to feed their children.

Rav Zundel Kroizer was a Vasikin Yid and he adopted the traits of the *talmidei chachamim* of *Yerushalayim shel Maalah*: he carried himself unpretentiously, and evaded those who tried to honor him.

An outstanding genius, Rav Zundel delved into the depths of Torah and unraveled its complexities. Nevertheless, when standing before his Creator, he davened slowly and carefully, with an endearing voice, like a young child yearning for his mother's attention.

He fled from honor and from all those who came from near and far asking for *berachos* and *yeshuos*. The few who merited to receive his *berachah* knew that a blessing given by this *gaon*, who serves his Creator with a pure heart, would never be returned unfulfilled.

סודה של חברותא

The Secret of the Chavrusa

There is a prevalent rumor in Yerushalayim claiming that a secret pact existed between Rav Zundel and Rav Gamliel Rabinowitz, *yibadel l'chaim aruchim*: Rav Zundel, author of *Ohr HaChamah,* taught Rav Gamliel the *niglah* of Torah, and Rav Gamliel, Rosh Yeshivah of the kabbalistic Yeshiva Sha'ar Hashamayim, taught Rav Zundel the *nistar* of Torah.

Rav Zundel humbly insisted on walking to the home of his *talmid-chaver* every day, and when the two of them secreted themselves to learn, nobody was allowed to stand near them.

Rav Zundel and Rav Gamliel sat in the living room of the house in Zichron Moshe, the ancient beauty of old *sefarim* and small letters hovering above them. Their minds were focused on the writings of the Arizal, Ramak, and Rabbeinu Chaim Vital, and the "*sod hapartzufim*" and "*heichalos*" would light up before them within the ancient writings. They whispered as they learned, because not every person is worthy of being exposed to the secrets of the Torah. Nobody could approach this holy scene. They sat alone — with their "*sefiros*" and their "*sodos*" as *seraphim* stood above them.

This picture provides a rare glimpse into the mysterious *seder limud*. Nobody will ever know what they learned, but everyone knows that the lofty angels created during their learning used their wings to shade the holy secrets that were rooted in the ground, but reached the heavens above.

במחיצת שקדן הדור

The Masmid of the Generation

The Gemara of Rabbeinu Yosef Shalom was like a string instrument waiting for a unique, sensitive finger that would know how to create sounds never heard before. When the Gaon of the generation sat and bonded with its letters, the Gemara fulfilled its purpose and generated *kedushah*.

Havdalah was recited about a half hour ago; the *neshamah yeseirah* has left. Rav Elyashiv's room is jam-packed with the young and old who heard his Havdalah, sang the special *tefillos* of Motza'ei Shabbos, and received a short *berachah*.

Even before the room was emptied, the *shtreimel* was back in its case resting on the bed he slumbered on for a short while every night, the Mekor HaBerachah siddur placed to the side. One last *berachah* for a small child, and the world returned to its regular course: the volume of Talmud was opened and enchanting sounds of Torah emanated from the room — a melody sung for one hundred years.

At times, when Rabbeinu Yosef Shalom reached *Maseches Shabbos*, *daf* 127, his melody caused every chord to vibrate. He sang to himself, never imagining that others were listening:

"*Shishah devarim…shishah…shishah…* there are six things…. *adam ochel peiroseihem ba'Olam HaZeh, v'hakeren kayemes lo la'Olam HaBa.*"

> **I was one of these children when I first went to *cheder*. The *melamed*, Rav Moshe Hershkowitz, sat me on his knees and taught me the letters of the aleph-beis. A great tzaddik who was present, Rav Moshe Weber, threw candies at me. When they told me it was the angel Gavriel who threw the candies, I believed them implicitly.**
>
> ("First Steps to Cheder," page 140)

Chapter Four
The Children of Yerushalayim

לילה של קְרִי׳שְׁמֶעְלֵיינֶען
The Night of Kriyas Shema

The children of Yerushalayim call the night before a *bris* "the night of *kri'shmeleinen*," because of the Kriyas Shema that is said by the crib of the baby boy then.

After returning from *cheder*, the boys wait impatiently until they go to the new baby's house. They knock once or twice until the happy, young father opens the door with a *Zohar* in his hand. "*Kumt arein*," he tells them, "*si'z da gute zachen*" (Come in, there are "good things" here). The children's eyes light up and they enter the living room where the baby is resting in his crib, eyes closed, hospital bracelet still on his hand. Tomorrow he will enter the *bris* of Avraham Avinu, but not before the children of Yerushalayim accept *ohl malchus Shamayim* around him.

The children stand and recite the first *parashah* of Shema. They have extra *kavanah* when saying the word "*echad*" — just as they were taught in *cheder*. They then recite *pesukim*, surrounded by the angels Michael, Gavriel, Raphael, and Uriel, while above the heads of these pure *tinokos shel beis raban* rests the Shechinah.

The cleverest boys will steal a glance or two toward the kitchen to spy out the "*gute zachen*" waiting for them: a *crembo* in the rainy season, a popsicle in the heat, or a fat *pekele* if, by some chance, the parents have a little more money in their pockets.

צעדים ראשונים ב'חיידר'

First Steps to Cheder

Wrapped in *talleisim* to protect their eyes from seeing anything impure and from an *ayin hara*, young sons are carried to *cheder* for the very first time by the fathers of Yerushalayim.

One hand holds his tallis-wrapped son and the other holds a honey cake (*honig lekach*), prepared by the boy's dedicated mother. The cake bears a message: Just as the honey cake is sweet to the palate, so too, my young son, the Torah that you start learning today is sweeter than anything else in the world.

Gedolei HaDoros said that the first time a child is brought to his rebbe is a great, lofty occasion. The Rebbe of Lubavitch (RaYaTz) *zt"l* said, "When a Jew gives his son to learn Torah, he accomplishes what the *Kohen Gadol* accomplished in the *Kodesh Hakedoshim*."

A festive table greets the three-year-old child in his rebbe's house. On the table are candies and treats, and a hard-boiled egg bearing a *pasuk* from *Yechezkel*. Next to the egg is the honey cake — decorated with a *pasuk* from *Yeshayah*.

The *melamed* places the young boy on his knees and begins teaching him the aleph-beis from a chart smeared with honey. The boy licks the honey, fulfilling the *pasuk* "*u'mesukim midvash ve'nofes tzufim*" — Torah is sweeter than honey.

I was one of these children when I first went to *cheder*. The *melamed*, Rav Moshe Hershkowitz, sat me on his knees and taught me the letters of the aleph-beis. A great tzaddik who was present, Rav Moshe Weber, threw candies at me. When they told me it was the angel Gavriel who threw the candies, I believed them implicitly.

Mrs. Yehudis Rubinstein *a"h*, a righteous woman, was also present. If there would be such a thing as "*lamed-vav tzaddikos*," she would be first on the list. She wasn't blessed with children of her own, and she spent her time reciting *Tehillim* and preparing food for needy families. She traveled all the way up to Meron for my *upsheren* and was there when I was brought to *cheder* for the first time.

She used to hum a Yiddish song, infused with *ahavas haTorah* and *emunah*:

עולם הבּא איז אַ גוטע זאַך

לערנען תורה איז די בעסטע זאַך

מאַך אַ מצווה מער און מער

לערן תורה נאָך און נאָך

עולם הבּא איז אַ גוטע זאַך.

The Children of Yerushalayim

צאן קודשים
HOLY FLOCK

"A *shureh*, make a line," announces the *melamed* of the *tinokos shel beis raban*, directing his young charges through the streets as they transition from nursery to their very first day in the first grade of *cheder*. To etch this event forever into their young hearts, the children begin *cheder* by marching through the neighborhood streets. Their teary-eyed mothers stand at a distance, watching their sons take their first steps in the world of Torah.

On the previous page, you can see the children of Toldos Aharon skipping through Salant Street. They are led by a young *melamed* who will teach them with the same devotion that he was taught as a child in Reb Simchah Breuer's class. "*A shureh, a shureh*," he continues shouting, and the children follow him like young sheep, happy and excited.

The picture, taken from Choni Hame'agel Street, echoes Meah Shearim: generations-old stones, and five-year-old children being educated between these stones and walls. Generations come and go, but the stones of Meah Shearim, in their unique way, stand forever.

הסוד של הַמּוֹיצְקַאלֶ׳ע
The Secret of the Moitzkal'eh

A deep secret is hidden between the slices of the Yerushalmi "*moitzkal'eh*."

Every day, when the Yerushalmi sun stands in the east and people are leaving for a day of work, the devoted Yerushalmi women wake their children and get them ready for a day of Torah study. The mothers turn to their *tinokos shel beis raban* and lovingly ask, "*Veleche moitzkal'eh vilstu?* — What type of sandwich do you want?" A *moitzkal'eh* is an affectionate name for a simple sandwich, per the rule that adding the suffix "*leh*" or "*keh*" to a word turns it into a term of endearment.

Yerushalmi children have lots of *moitzkal'eh*: "*moitzkal'eh mit chocolad*," bread with chocolate spread; "*moitzkal'eh mit kez*," bread with cheese; or "*shires mit tamates*," bread dipped in oil and tomato juice — the choice for those who make do with little.

I always chose the "*moitzkal'eh mit chocolad*" when I was young, and though the neighborhood dentist berated me for my blackened teeth, he earned a nice living from my lunch.

The children in this picture learn in Toldos Aharon. Although they are surrounded by peeling walls and antiquated metal windows, the most important thing is that they have a *melamed* and not, *chalilah*, a nursery school "*morah*." The *melamed* teaches them the aleph-beis, reads *pesukim* from *Tehillim* together with them, and sings "*tov li Toras picha*," "*ve'sen banu yetzer tov*," and other songs that inspire little children to *yiras Shamayim*. The *melamdim* are also filled with *yiras Shamayim*; it's said that this profession is a proven *segulah* for perfecting one's *middos*, even when off-duty.

And what is the secret of the sandwich? Whether it's a *moitzkal'eh* smeared with chocolate, filled with cheese, or dipped in oil and tomatoes, the sandwich is always spiced with the tears of the Yerushalmi mother, who davens that her son grow in Torah and *yiras Shamayim*.

בזכות הבל פיהם

Pure Merit

There's nobody like Rebbe Lipshitz: that's the contention of the Toldos Aharon *avreichim* who learned to read by Reb Avrum Lipshitz, sent their sons to Rebbe Lipshitz, and now have grandchildren learning by Rebbe Lipshitz. Rebbe Lipshitz is ready to teach the fourth and even fifth generation to read — as long as he's blessed with days and years.

Rebbe Lipshitz is an esteemed member of the Karlin Chassidus, has hundreds of descendants, and dedicates parts of his day to campaigns regarding *kedushah*. But above all, his primary desire is to lovingly teach Jewish children. He doesn't want to move up to an administrative position. He's not looking for wealth or a promotion. Born a *melamed*, a *melamed* he will remain, and as a *melamed* he will greet Mashiach.

Rebbe Lipshitz keeps a notebook hidden in his drawer in which he records the progress of each and every *talmid*.

A *talmid* read a whole page? He receives a *"lieb frask,"* a loving pat.

בַּכִּתָּה שֶׁל רֶבֶּ'ה לִיפְשִׁיץ
In Rebbe Lipshitz's Class

Rebbe Lipshitz is very patient — as patient as Hillel who was bothered on Erev Shabbos *bein hashemashos* but didn't get angry. Rebbe Lipshitz tolerates children's antics and never complains about impulsive, childish tricks.

A bazooka-flavored snuff case rests in his pocket. Why? Because the sense of smell is enjoyed by the *neshamah* — not the body. His beard is stained yellow from years of sniffing snuff and a boy who excels and receives a pinch of snuff from Rebbe Lipshitz is the happiest person in the world.

Rebbe Lipshitz will teach a child even one hundred times until he absorbs his studies like a *bor sud* — a well that doesn't lose even a drop of water. When he wants to make his little students happy, he puts a funny hat on his head — anything to increase the joy in the hearts of *tinokos shel beis raban*. A student who merits a chocolate from Rebbe Lipshitz is filled with unparalleled joy.

Rebbe Lipshitz's brother, a Yerushalmi construction contractor, offered him a job in the business so that he could earn a lucrative living. But Rebbe Lipshitz turned him down: a *melamed* he is and a *melamed* he will remain.

הרב'ה שלימדני תורה
The Rebbe Who Taught Me Torah

Twenty-five years have passed since I learned aleph-beis by Rebbe Cheshin. During those twenty-five years governments changed and earthquakes shook the world. The generation of facsimiles and snail-mail was replaced with the generation of insane virtual addiction — and the innocence of my childhood is no longer what it was.

But my *melamed* is still doing what he did forty years ago: walking every morning to *cheder* to greet his five-year-old students. This is the third generation that is learning aleph-beis in his class, yet he teaches them with the exuberance of a fresh, young *melamed*.

His name is Reb Avraham Cheshin. We called him "Rebbe Cheshin," and I don't recall if we even knew his first name when I was learning my first syllables. Today, Rebbe Cheshin is armed with the same resolute stride, the same determination in his eyes, and perhaps even the same bag with the same towel that he used to bring with him to *cheder*.

I once met Rebbe Cheshin when I was a married man. I excitedly indentified myself and we exchanged a few words. "So I guess you finally learned how to read — and even to write, *nu?*" he quipped. His little joke sharpened the realization that, for him, nothing had changed over the years; but for me, nothing remained as it was.

For one small moment, I felt like a five-year-old practicing to read from a *Sefer Hamesores*. I was reminded of my pure childhood and thought nostalgically about my lost innocence. Though Rebbe Cheshin remembered me well, he wasn't overly sentimental: meeting grown men whom he had once taught was an everyday occurrence for him.

When I parted from my rebbe, I thought about his straight posture and the pride and satisfaction that he had in his position. He truly felt that his was the most prestigious profession one could ever dream of.

As he walked away, I thought about our generation: Today, some *melamdim* don't think highly of their vocation. They see their job as second-class, reserved for those who didn't succeed at anything else.

If only, I said to myself, more Rebbe Cheshins would sprout up among us.

הֶבֶל פִּיהֶם שֶׁל תִּינוֹקוֹת
Sweet Words

In Yerushalmi *chadorim*, the end of the day is used to read *pesukim* written by the *Ne'im Zemiros Yisrael*, David Hamelech. This has a few benefits: First of all, there is no greater virtue than pure children reading *Tehillim*; it defeats the enemy, heals the sick, and generates salvation. Secondly, it's an effective method of reading practice. And third, this is when the children start to yawn. Their level of concentration declines and they have a harder time delving into more intricate studies.

The décor in this picture is typical of Yerushalmi *chadorim*: an old metal cabinet with a heavy lock stands behind the rebbe's chair and is lovingly decorated with pictures and texts that benefit the young disciples.

This particular *melamed* is Rebbe Blum, an *avreich* from Toldos Aharon. Just like all Yerushalmi *melamdim*, if he sees a young *talmid* sleeping at this point, he doesn't wake him. Sweet is the sleep of the Yerushalmi child who slumbers over his books at four o'clock in the afternoon. Truth be told, the rebbe is also a little tired. If he could, he would also take a nap....

Any moment, the redeeming bell will sound, and the children will cheerfully go home.

תכף יישמע הצלצול
Listen for the Bell!

The purity of the children of the Yishuv Hayashan is one of the most touching wonders of the world. These children are free of the pollution and inanities of the street and are proud of their lack of familiarity with the outside world.

They wake up early. The *"chevras tefillah"* starts at seven o'clock in the morning, and after that they're in the care of their *melamed*. Whether a young *avreich* or an elderly man, the *melamed* invests his energies into being *mechanech* the children to Torah and Yiddishkeit. Never does an elderly Yerushalmi answer *"pahst nisht"* to a teaching position. He lovingly accepts the opportunity to educate *tinokos shel beis raban*.

The schedule of a boy in the Yishuv Hayashan is different than the schedule of one who isn't Yerushalmi. Recesses are short, he never heard of summer vacation, and he doesn't dare talk about a trip out loud, lest the *Mashgiach* kick him out. Even during recess, he has a very limited choice of games: hide-and-seek, *kugelach*, and a sharp trade in apricot pits, called *"Ajuim."*

Especially charming are the children of Toldos Aharon, who are even more pure than the typical Yerushalmi child. They speak only Yiddish and are educated *"al taharas hakodesh."* Their *melamdim* are usually *avreichim* from within their own community, and secular subjects are taught only minimally — just what they need in order to read and write and do simple math equations.

The Yerushalmi *cheder* finishes at six o'clock in the evening, but after the bell rings, you can occasionally find a child fast asleep. He slumbers over his *Tehillim*— sweetness on top of sweetness.

Look at this picture: Is there any other place in the world where such purity can be found? Precious is the sleep of the child in the Yerushalmi *cheder* who toils over Torah from morning until night.

הַקַדְצ'קֶה של רֶבֶּה שִׂמְחָהלֶ'ה
Rebbe Simcha'le's Kadotskeh

The dialect of Yerushalmi children differs from that of children in the rest of the world.

If this can be said about regular Meah Shearim children, it is sevenfold truer of the "Reb Aharele" children, who are guarded as carefully as *esrogim* in flax fibers by *"der rebbe fun cheder,"* under the strict guidance of *"der Rebbe fun shul."* (That's how the children differentiate between the Admor and their *cheder melamed*.)

At least two generations of children have passed through the hands of rebbe Simcha'le Breuer, the first-grade *rebbe*. He lives up to his name: he brims with cheerfulness and can deftly move his legs in a frenzied Kadotskeh dance at a *simchas beis hashoeivah* or in Meron.

To refresh his students, he takes them out to the lot in front of the *cheder* and sings with them, using a high-decibel megaphone — as seen in this picture.

The Ministry of Education can be seen in the background. Just a few feet separate the building that administrates the entire government-run educational system and the autonomous education of the Reb Aharelech: just a few feet, but hundreds of light-years.

מציצים מן החרכים
Peeking through the Cracks

"*Der tender kumt*," the Yerushalmi children say as they leave *cheder*, like the proverbial child running away from school. They merrily climb into a rickety, hot box of tin with unupholstered benches. The windows are covered with amateur-made security bars — the only things that separate the children from the world outside.

One Talmud Torah in the Yishuv Hayashan is nothing like the next: the children in the Etz Chaim Talmud Torah are blessed with mischievousness while the children of Toldos Aharon are known for their naïve affability and purity.

When one school van draws close to another, the children shout at each other. Each van is proud of its particular school and chides the children in the passing van for lacking the merit of learning there.

The words on a Yerushalmi *cheder* van never correspond to the *cheder* that the children actually learn in. If the van says "Beis Yisrael," the children riding it learn in "Etz Chaim." If it says "Etz Chaim," it probably transports the *cheder* children of "Shomrei Hachomos," and so on. What is the reason? We don't know, but one thing's for sure: *al tistakel bakankan* — look not at the van, but at its passengers: enchanting, clever *cheder* children.

עגלה, יַרְמוּלְקֶ'ה וְקַאפֶּעלוּש

Carriage, Yarmulke, and Kapelush

The large, blessed families of the Yishuv Hayashan expect their children to behave maturely, even when they're young. It's not uncommon to see a five-year-old girl pushing a carriage with her one-year-old brother, as if she is a young Jewish mother instead of a toddler herself. When she's not helping with her siblings, the Yerushalmi girl practices with her doll carriage, preparing herself for the not-so-far-off day, in about thirteen years, when she herself will become a Jewish mother. And if she still sucks a pacifier — who cares?

חכמת ילדי ירושלים

Clever Yerushalmi Children

Yerushalmi children are fundamentally mischievous and have a plethora of improvised tricks that were spawned by a lack of playground equipment and conventional toys.

One of their games is the "cup game": An experienced child holds a broom with two cups of water. He spins the broom quickly and acrobatically, like the propeller of a helicopter. (Not that the children of Meah Shearim have ever been in a helicopter, *rachmana litzlan*. Anything hinting at *kochi v'otzem yadi* is an anathema to them. They soar only with the Torah and their faith in Hashem.)

שלא תשלוט העין

Bli Ayin Hara

Yerushalmi mothers precede each mention of their children with the words *"kein ayin hara."* In this particular point, Yerushalmi women are very similar to the mothers of the *Eidot Mizrach*: they are very careful regarding *ayin hara*s lest they impact their children.

If a mother suspects that an *ayin hara* caught hold of her child, she immediately goes to the elderly women in Yerushalayim who know the secrets of the *"ois'shprechin"* incantation. To do an *ois'shprechin*, a piece of lead is melted in a pan on the fire. The melted lead is poured into a bowl of water placed on the head of the child — of course, there's a towel between the head and the bowl of water in case, *chas v'shalom*, the bowl overturns.

While the melted lead is in the bowl of water, the elderly Yerushalmi women recite incantations until it takes on the shape of an eye. This is the *ayin hara* that has left the child's body.

This may also be the reason why Yerushalmi women take their children to see fish when it's time for *tashlich*. The meaning is: Just like these fish are sheltered from the eyes of people and aren't affected by *ayin hara*, so too, may you be guarded from evil eyes, and may we merit to raise you to Torah and the chuppah.

בעגלה ובזמן קריב

Wagon Country

On principle, the Jerusalem municipality rarely places playground equipment in Meah Shearim. This is based on an unwritten agreement of separation between the local authorities and the neighborhood.

What do the children of Meah Shearim do without parks and playgrounds? You can be sure they don't allow themselves to get bored. That's what carriages were made for — baby carriages and shopping carts make great toys. And if the carriage is broken and tied to a pole, what difference does it make?

צדיק גדול יהיה

Little Tzaddik

It is said that ten measures of shrewd innocence came down to the world and nine were taken by the children of the Yishuv Hayashan. They were then granted the tenth in this merit.

You may ask: Can innocence and shrewdness blend? Yes! They join forces in an incomprehensible way until you visit *Yerushalayim shel Maalah* and witness innocent children carrying out cunning pranks.

From the time they are small, they yearn to be great. They're taught to denigrate the materialistic world we live in, to be disgusted by the culture prevalent outside and to nullify every foreign influence — including the Hebrew language. In this way, they're educated in the traditions of their grandfathers and great-grandfathers who followed this way of life. Other than the passing of a few calendar years, there is no environmental or cultural difference between this generation and generations past.

Baruch Yaari once noticed the laundry hanging in the big courtyard in Batei Rand (after all, the women of this neighborhood would never allow themselves to become dependent on the services of the modern dryer!). Among the flapping clothes was a little bib. The embroidered text encapsulated the prayers of the loving mother: *"kleiner tzaddik"* — little tzaddik. This small tzaddik will indeed become a great tzaddik one day.

כבסים של קודש

Holy Laundry

The Reb Aharelech children wear white yarmulkes, artistically knitted with woven designs that are passed down by *mesorah*.

Expert Yerushalmi women knit these yarmulkes by hand so the children and their parents can wear them. One such yarmulke knitter was the great *tzadekes* Mrs. Yehudis Rubinstein *a"h*, a woman of *chesed* who knit gorgeous yarmulkes and *gartlech*. Masses streamed to her house of *chesed* in Batei Ungarin to buy a fitting yarmulke.

Yerushalmi children wear *tallis katan*s made of dark woven material. They wear them on top of their clothes; the dark color hides the dirt they play in and the chocolate from their *moitzkal'eh*. Even though the tzitzis are dark, they still need to be washed every few days and hung in the central courtyard of Batei Ungarin, above the ancient cistern near the Kesav Sofer Shul.

ממיתין עצמם עליה
With All Your Soul

At eight o'clock in the evening, some Meah Shearim children enter the shul in Batei Neitin to review what they learned with Rav Steinharter *zt"l*, an elderly *talmid chacham*.

Despite their young age, these children passionately desire to grow in Torah. Disregarding the fact that they've already put in a long day of learning, they happily come, leaving games and playmates behind.

Despite the disparity of age and status, Rav Steinharter learns with the young sheep.

The shul in Batei Neitin is wrapped in the glory of yesteryear. Rav Steinharter's *ahavas haTorah* rests in a corner, available to anyone who wants to come and take as much as he can carry. Boys interested in supplementing their diligence with more diligence go to learn with Rav Steinharter — not for prizes and not because they're forced to go.

They go because in Yerushalayim there are children who take their Torah studies very seriously. They learn day and night, even while yawning with tears of tiredness in the corners of their eyes during this study session that's tacked on to their regular *cheder* day.

Torah is acquired only by those who dedicate their lives to it — and this includes children.

"

On Tu bi'Shevat, the righteous women of Batei Ungarin are already seen cleaning their homes for Pesach. They clean and polish a little bit every day, full of joy for the mitzvah without the slightest grievance. By Rosh Chodesh Nissan their homes are scrubbed and rubbed, shining in their simple glory. The whitewash on the ceiling might be peeling, the bare walls crying for a new coat of paint, the floor worn out and faded; nevertheless, more beautiful is the rickety home of the righteous Yerushalmi woman than a palace with shining marble, sparkling chandeliers and alabaster floors.

("Sweating for a Mitzvah," page 197)

CHAPTER FIVE
The Month of Nissan

שלא חיסר בעולמו

BLESSING ON THE FRUIT TREES

Yerushalmis glorify anything related to *"birkas ha'ilanos"* that's recited upon the arrival of the month of Nissan, when the sun generously bestows light and warmth upon the whole world, since it's springtime — *Chodesh Ha'aviv*.

On the first of Nissan, right after davening of Rosh Chodesh, the *anshei Yerushalayim* go out to the gardens and orchards to recite the *berachah* of *"Shelo chi'ser ba'olamo klum."* They bless and thank Hashem for creating a world filled with creatures and trees for human beings to enjoy. Some Yerushalmis even merge two mitzvos: they draw water for *mayim she'lanu* for matzos from the Sataf Stream and recite the *birkas ha'ilanos* on nearby fruit trees.

Right after Rosh Chodesh davening, Maran Rabbeinu Yosef Shalom walked to the Shaarei Chesed neighborhood and joyfully made a *berachah* on the different types of fruit trees that sprout, bud, and flower in Hakadosh Baruch Hu's perfect world.

בשקתות המים

Going to the Source

Just before the evening shadows of the fourteenth day of Nissan, the Chassidim go to the gurgling streams in the Walaja Valley in the south of Yerushalayim, or the slopes of Motza in the west of the city, to draw *mayim she'lanu* for *matzos mitzvah*. These matzos are different from regular matzos; they will be eaten at the Seder to fulfill the *mitzvas asei mid'Oraisa*.

In these pictures, the men of Toldos Aharon, middle-aged and older, despite their waning strength and advanced age, are drawing water in buckets. They do the physical work on their own, heeding the words of our Sages that it is better for a person to do the mitzvah himself than to appoint a representative.

Right before *plag haMinchah* of the fourteenth day of Nissan, these people of action bake matzos *l'shem mitzvah* after *chatzos* — to commemorate the Korban Pesach that was sacrificed after midday. These *matzos shel mitzvah* are very costly, but nobody complains. The efforts and cost involved are an expression of their love for the mitzvah.

After procuring three precious *matzos mitzvah*, a Yerushalmi returns home with his children, happy and satisfied, properly prepared for the Pesach Seder.

השרפים לבית בריסק
The Seraphim of Brisk

Brisk: the word arouses pre- and mis-conceptions about a world of stringencies and stern faces. But here's the truth: anyone who makes light conversation with a Brisker lion is captivated by the serenity that replaces the nervous seriousness that characterizes his mitzvah performance.

On *Motza'ei* Shivah Asar b'Tammuz 2012, I visited the home of Rav Meir Soloveitchik *zt"l*, Rosh Yeshivah of Brisk and son of the Brisker Rav *zt"l*. Crossing that threshold on Chazanovitz Street was like hopping over to a new continent: whatever interests the world outside is of no interest to the people living under this roof and, conversely, the subjects enjoyed in this home do not interest the unrefined masses outside. When I came in, a mug of tea with a sugar cube stood in front of Rav Meir, who was wearing a light blue dressing gown and a Brisker hat.

Rav Meir looked astonishingly like his father. He was a perfect blend of *charifus* and refinement. His strict adherence to the fine points of halachah in no way contradicted his gracious warmth. His words, though sharp, dripped with nectar.

His words were thought-out and deliberate, his face illuminated. He never exaggerated his descriptions, but stuck to the truth. In Brisk, there is only truth and the truth guides the way. "In Brisk," he told me back then, "we don't care about political parties. If you're a *yerei Shamayim*, *baruch haba* — welcome."

In the opposite picture, Rav Meir stands next to his brother, Rav Meshulam Dovid *shlita*, and his brother-in-law, Rav Yaakov Schiff *shlita*, the son-in-law of the Brisker Rav *zy"a*. He's pouring water for his matzos with the Brisker stringency, yet without any contradiction to his serenity and the pleasantness of his ways.

מצה זו שאנו אופים
Only the Best

In Toldos Aharon, the business of baking matzah is reserved for the *avreichim*, with *yiras Shamayim* beating in their hearts, pure Chassidus shining on their faces, and without a cellphone in their pockets (unless it's a "kosher" phone *l'mehadrin*). These *avreichim* take a break from their regular Torah studies during the weeks leading up to Pesach in order to earn some *parnassah* from baking matzos.

The work is hard; turning a matzah into a flat sheet isn't the easiest job. They are very meticulous as to the fine points of baking matzah, ensuring that there isn't even the slightest suspicion of *chametz*.

זיעה של מצווה
Sweating for a Mitzvah

On Tu bi'Shevat, the righteous women of Batei Ungarin are already seen cleaning their homes for Pesach. They clean and polish a little bit every day, full of joy for the mitzvah without the slightest grievance. By Rosh Chodesh Nissan their homes are scrubbed and rubbed, shining in their simple glory. The whitewash on the ceiling might be peeling, the bare walls crying for a new coat of paint, the floor worn out and faded; nevertheless, more beautiful is the rickety home of the righteous Yerushalmi woman than a palace with shining marble, sparkling chandeliers, and alabaster floors.

The white pom-pommed yarmulke-wearing children of Toldos Aharon never pass up the chance to participate in the cleaning. Walk through Yerushalmi neighborhoods before Pesach and the pungent fragrance of cleansers will penetrate your lungs, testifying to the cleaning and scrubbing all around.

The *akeres bayis* orchestrates the fevered cleaning like a battle-decorated general who nobody dares contradict. She tells Yankele to polish the *leichters* and Yossel to clean the "*kanapeh*" (the tablecloth). Dovid is told to paddle the upholstery on the "*beinklach*" (chairs) and the "*perineh*" (blanket), until not a vestige of rebellious dust can be detected.

On the left, you can see cute, obedient Duvidel paddling the chairs with a face as red as a fully ripe tomato, radiating the joy of the mitzvah.

בדרך לחֲלוּקֶע
On the Way to "Chalukah"

In Yerushalayim, Pesach cleaning is not determined by age, gender, or status. Everybody works hard to fulfill the mitzvah of *"tashbisu s'or mibateichem"* — even young children. Sometimes tasks are invented just for the sake of *chinuch*, like the kid pushing the *sponga* stick in the courtyard or the other kid cleaning the classroom window. The Romanian cleaner will clean the Talmud Torah again afterwards, but the smell of this cleaning job will forever be stamped on the child's heart.

While the little kids help their mothers clean, the fathers and older brothers run between the different *"chalukahs"* — distribution points. During this period of the big *chalukahs*, many Yerushalmis leave their homes as soon as the sun rises, full of strength and vigor. They take carriages to carry their heavy burdens and enthusiastically go about their *chalukah*-catching campaign.

The experienced *"chalukah* catchers" hurry to Stern's *Chalukah* in the morning where quality *kartuflach* (potatoes) await them. They're not interested in what remains by the end of the day — a sparse selection of banged-up, oddly-shaped potatoes. From Stern's *Chalukah,* they go to Chasdei Yitzchak; from there they continue on to the *Chalukah* of their Chassidus; and for dessert, they proceed to a little-known boutique *chalukah* that liberally doles out more potatoes.

הגעלה של מצווה

Scouring the Pots

Though this scene is not unique to Erev Pesach in the Knesset Yisrael neighborhood, Knesset is still special. The neighborhood is planted in the center of Yerushalayim, in a place called "the Shtetlach" by the *chareidi*m of the Yishuv Hayashan and "Nachlaot" by the general public.

Look at the purity in the faces of the children as they bring utensils from home to the shul's yard, per the instructions of their righteous mothers. In the yard is a giant vat of bubbling, boiling water. Next to the vat is a tub of cold water.

The paid worker places the utensils inside the basket and immerses them in the boiling water in order to dislodge any vestiges of *chametz*. The utensils are then quickly dunked into the cold water. The utensils are now *kosher l'mehadrin*, worthy of being used at the royal table on Pesach night.

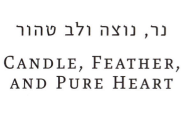

נר, נוצה ולב טהור
Candle, Feather, and Pure Heart

Two weeks before the fourteenth day of the month of Nissan, the Yerushalmi women make their kitchens kosher for Pesach so they can begin to cook scrumptious food for the seven days of Yom Tov. Creatively and heroically, they work with the minute amount of products that enter Yerushalmi kitchens on Pesach. A giant tin vat stands in the center of the kitchen. The vat is filled with cold, filtered water that lasts from Erev Pesach until after Pesach; after all, perhaps the water of the Kinneret has *chametz* in it.

The eve of *bedikas chametz* is an emotional time. The fragrance of gefilte fish emanates from the kitchen; the counter is covered with thin layers of tin, adding their own touch to the Pesach feeling.

The father makes a *berachah* and inspects the worn-but-shining tiles and the corroded-but-meticulously-scrubbed cabinets. A candle, a feather, and a wooden spoon are in his hands, his eyes shining, his essence proclaiming joy for the mitzvah.

In this sparkling and polished house that's *mehadrin min hamehadrin*, months of toil and sweat and endless water and cleansers culminate in the fulfillment of *bedikas chametz*.

בחורים ובסדקים

In the Holes and Cracks

Those meticulous in mitzvah performance spare no energy when it comes to *bedikas chametz*. They bend under cabinets, climb on top of them, rummage in the holes, and search in the cracks. Pictured is Rav Ben Tzion Gutfarb stooping underneath the table in his kitchen. Despite his age and stature, he toils with all his strength, searching for *chametz* by the light of the candle.

In the picture on the facing page, Rav Mordechai Aharon Sheinberger zt"l, a Yerushalmi Torah legend who had every single statement in the Torah stored in his mind, has his Gemara closed as he joyfully inspects his home to fulfill the commandment of *"'v'lo yeira'eh l'cha chametz."*

שריפת חמץ של רבי שמעון
Rav Shimon's Sreifas Chametz

Rav Shimon Yakobovitz zt"l, Rav Aryeh Levin's oldest grandson, strode with a pure heart to the thorned and thisteled lot next to his house in Batei Wittenberg. He held some scraps in his hands, including leftover *chametz*, a candle and feather, and the ten pieces of bread that his righteous wife, a scion of the Yerushalmi Kroizer family, had hid in scattered corners of their home.

Rav Shimon was always submerged in learning, which often generated some impatience with the world and its absurdities. He waged a perpetual battle against the clock; it threatened to prevent him from finishing his daily *shiurim* — sprinkled with Tanach, Mishnah, Gemara, halachah, *aggadah*, Chassidish *ma'amarim*, and other studies culled from all topics in the Torah.

On Erev Pesach, however, his face exuded a rare look of tranquility, as if he had finished all of his Torah studies until Pesach's arrival.

At the start of the fifth hour, he walked complacently to the field and lit a fire with a pile of twigs and a fat *Hamodia* newspaper. Joyfully, he threw his crumbs into the blaze, making sure they were completely consumed by the fire, to fulfill the mitzvah of *"tashbisu."*

As the fire burned, he took a siddur *Tehillas Hashem* and read from it with great concentration. The children of Batei Wittenberg are looking on admiringly as he nullifies his *chametz*.

כָּל חֲמִירָא וַחֲמִיעָא דְּאִיכָּא בִרְשׁוּתִי,
דְּלָא חֲמִתֵּיהּ, וּדְלָא בְעַרְתֵּיהּ,
וּדְלָא יְדַעְנָא לֵיהּ, לִבָּטֵל וְלֶהֱוֵי
הֶפְקֵר כְּעַפְרָא דְאַרְעָא.

כעפרא דארעא

As the Dust of the Earth

Morning on Erev Pesach is a special time in the Yishuv Hayashan. Its distinguished residents wake up early and rush to eat a *k'zayis* of *chametz* minutes before taking leave of the *chametz* or anything resembling it — and anything that may resemble something that looks like *chametz*.

After shaking out their clothes, the residents of Batei Ungarin make a bonfire in the "Ungarishe Feld" (the Hungarian Field) behind the neighborhood. Here they burn all leftover *chametz* — usually pitas that could not be finished in time and were left outside, near their homes. Because that's what they do: About two weeks before Pesach, these distinguished Yerushalmis leave their homes at mealtime and eat outside behind a strip of tarp or a sheet that is no longer serviceable as a sheet. Hung on a laundry line, the tarp or sheet provides privacy during lunchtime, ensuring that they're not, *chalilah*, likened to a dog who eats in the street.

In the picture on the facing page stands Rav Meir Bransdorfer *zt"l* as he burns his *chametz* in the field behind the Batei Ungarin neighborhood.

הכול מעלין לזופניק
Everyone Goes to Zupnik

*C*hareidi Jewry of the Yishuv Hayashan is administrated from the second floor of the Zupnik Buildings on Strauss Street, behind the porch used for demonstrations and *levayos*. For years it has housed the *Beis Din,* which influences fate, discusses *dinei Torah,* and decides which campaigns *chareidi* Jewry will take up as their cause. This is the site throughout the year where *dinei Torah* and stormy communal meetings take place, where each *dayan* fearlessly expresses his opinion. But once a year, on the fourteenth of Nissan, the narrow room is home to a special ceremony. A few minutes before "*sof zeman biur chametz,*" the senior *dayanim* sit facing an Arab from Sha'ar Shechem who has a decades-long *chazakah* of buying *chametz* from the *dayanim* of the Eidah HaChareidis.

The ceremony is carried out in Hebrew, a language familiar to both parties. The *dayanim* review each clause and explain the details of the sale — as if they hadn't explained the same thing last year and won't repeat it again next year. The task of explaining the clauses was usually assumed by Rav Yisrael Yaakov Fisher *zt"l,* the legendary *dayan* and Torah giant, who was also well-versed in the practicalities of daily life and human behavior.

Troops of curious people cram the *Beis Din* during the sale. This is one of the few ceremonies open to the public — unlike the giving of a *get, chalitzah,* or a complicated *din Torah,* which take place behind closed doors to protect the privacy of those involved. When the ceremony is concluded, the Arab goes out, happy and satisfied, and the *dayanim* are free once again to discuss public issues. They are now available to sign placards and posters being readied for Chol HaMoed — informing and educating the public, and protesting against any breaches made in the spiritual walls of the Yishuv Hayashan.

In this picture, from right to left, are the irreplaceable, unforgettable senior *dayanim,* the great *Geonim* Rav Moshe Halberstam, Rav Yaakov Blau, Rav Yisrael Yaakov Fisher, and Rav Meir Bransdorfer, *zecher tzaddikim v'geonim livrachah,* and Rav Avraham Yitzchak Ulman, *yibadel l'chaim aruchim.*

אפיקומן גדול ואפיקומנים קטנים

The Big Afikomen and the Small Afikomens

The Seder experience for a child in a Yerushalmi *cheder* is strong and sweet. Thirty days prior to the Yom Tov, the rebbe begins practicing the Mah Nishtanah with Yiddish *teitsch*: "*Tateh*," the boy will begin the questions at the Seder, "*ich vil dir fregen de fir kashes*" (Father, I want to ask you the four questions).

The children learn about the Pesach Seder starting with

"*Kadesh*" and ending in "*Nirtzah.*" Each *siman* has a Yiddish explanation and added elucidations regarding its essence so that the Seder should be an experiential event for the child, whose pockets will be stuffed with "*klayos and egozim*" or, as they're better known, "*nisselech mit mandelech.*"

A special love and devotion is reserved for the *chinuch* of the children of the Yishuv — just as the *matzah shmura*h is guarded from the time it's cut and like the *afikomen* of Pesach night.

The children are preserved in their purity, just as they were when they were born, with no exposure to the inanities of this world. Just like this *afikomen* is hidden and guarded and watched, so too, every single child is an *afikomen* in his own right.

These are the children in the Toldos Aharon *cheder*. Their rebbe wears a white *kittel* in order to create an experiential Pesach Seder and prepare his young students for the great, holy day.

למטה מן השטריימל

Under the *Shtreimel*

A Yerushalmi child is guarded like an *esrog* wrapped in flax fibers, protected against the harmful effects of the street, and guarded against the foreign winds that blow outside.

A halo of purity rests on the faces of these children — they've never tasted the taste of sin nor heard its voice. Their speech, talk, and appearance is different than that of children in the rest of the world, enveloping them in an aura of wholesome purity. This is especially true of the children of Toldos Aharon, most of whom are named Ahre'le or Avraham Yitzchak — after the patriarchs of this stringent Chassidus. Nothing compares to the sweet, triumphant smiles of these children standing in the school yard, as if mocking and ridiculing the entire world.

They are proud of their conservatism and lack of familiarity with the world and its follies. They're told of the iniquities of the wicked people of the world, and although they may despise their deeds, they answer pleasantly to anyone in the street who addresses them. The Yerushalmi child is not shy or hesitant; he is proud, mischievous to some extent, and pities the rest of the world.

On the Shabbos before his bar mitzvah, the Yerushalmi boy starts wearing a *shtreimel* (usually one inherited from an older brother who received a new one in honor of his marriage). If he is a Chassid of Toldos Aharon, he will also wear a silk garment with gold stripes.

The minute he dons these clothes, he is a grown-up, a *"mitzuveh v'oseh,"* fulfilling the mitzvos of his Creator per the path that his forefathers paved.

מגודלים בנעוריהם
Children, Don't Go Too Far

"Megudalim Bin'ureihem" is the Yerushalmi children's organization run by Reb Ureh (Uri) Blau, the son and successor of Rav Amram the *Kanai*.

The organization's main goal is to guard the pure children of Yerushalayim from everything in the outside world. Generations change and move on, trends start and fade, but the children of Yerushalayim continue to go to Megudalim Bin'ureihem.

On Lag Ba'Omer, the children of Megudalim Bin'ureihem participate in a gathering that shields them from other dubious and untrustworthy parades. Reb Ureh distributes copies of "Bar Yochais" — the *piyut* "*Bar Yochai, nimshachta ashrecha*" — printed on long, thin pieces of paper.

The primary goal of the organization is apparent at Pesach time, when the children of Yerushalayim travel to greet the *Gaon Av Beis Din* of Yerushalayim and bask in his presence. Buses then take them to recite the *berachah* on flowering fruit trees in Ramat Rachel at the edge of Yerushalayim. From there, they go to the promenade in Armon HaNetziv in order to view the Makom HaMikdash; today, they see the gold dome that, due to our great sins, has replaced it. They also see the Kosel, which, according to the *kanaim*, should only be seen from a distance.

Reb Shmuel Aryeh Markowitz, Reb Uri's son-in-law, announces through the megaphone, *"Kinder nisht gein veit —* Children, don't go too far." This warning has a few implications.

With one stern look, Reb Shmuel Aryeh can effectively discipline a child, whether he learns in Shomrei Hachomos where Reb Shmuel Aryeh serves as *Mashgiach* or whether he learns anywhere else in Yerushalayim. This is an entertaining trip for Yerushalmi children and it fills them with joy.

"

From generations back, the Cheshin family has a *chazakah* on the *hadlakah* in Batei Wittenberg. This bonfire is made of wood piled stories high by the Yerushalmi children and their parents; collection of the wood begins the minute that Pesach ends.

("Lighting Performs the Mitzvah," page 229)

CHAPTER SIX

Lag Ba'Omer

אש תמיד תוקד

HOLY FLAMES

Lag Ba'Omer is the holiday of Yerushalmi children. From a young age, *cheder* children enjoy the bonfires their rebbes light for them, often necessitating a bit of creativity. One *melamed* uses a can of whitewash placed on top of a discarded washing machine and another fills an industrial-sized pan with old *shmatteh*s soaked in kerosene. The *hadlakah* in the pan is the *hadlakah* of Toldos Aharon. The *hadlakah* on the washing machine is that of Toldos Avraham Yitzchak.

Whether the fire is in a can of whitewash or an industrial-sized frying pan, the goal is to educate Jewish children in the light of the *Tanna HaEloki*. In either case, the general rule in

all Yerushalmi *chadorim* is "don't look at the outside container, but at the fire burning within it," because the children of Yerushalayim are drawn to flames of mitzvos and delight in watching the holy fires ignited in honor of Bar Yochai.

Shomrei Hachomos organizes an early bonfire as well. This Talmud Torah, founded by Hungarian immigrants, has students from all factions of the Yishuv Hayashan. On Erev Lag Ba'Omer, Rav Avraham Cheshin, a *melamed* who has taught aleph-beis to four generations, makes an impressive *hadlakah* atop an overturned pot.

At the bottom of the wide windows, facing the shul named for the Chasam Sofer, the children sit in rows and, with radiant faces, sing "Bar Yochai."

When the *cheder* starts filling up with smoke, the *melamed* puts out the fire. The children are disappointed, but this is also an educational lesson: *chamira sakanta mei'isura*.

הדלקה עושה מצווה

Lighting Performs the Mitzvah

Hadlakah oseh mitzvah. In Yerushalayim this is true not only of the Chanukah *hadlakah* discussed in the *Shulchan Aruch*, but also of the *hadlakah* of Lag Ba'Omer, transmitted by *mesorah* for generations.

In Yerushalayim, it's not just energetic young children who prepare for the bonfire, but also adults. In addition, Yerushalmis don't make do with discarded pieces of wood, but spend money to purchase cotton and pure olive oil in honor of the *Tanna HaEloki*.

From generations back, the Cheshin family has a *chazakah* on the *hadlakah* in Batei Wittenberg. This bonfire is made of wood piled stories high by the Yerushalmi children and their parents; collection of the wood begins the minute that Pesach ends. Here, on the right, is Rav Dovid Cheshin. On the left is Rav Ben Tzion Gutfarb, his face reflecting the flames of the Batei Wittenberg *hadlakah*.

וזה מעשה המנורה

Preparing the Menorah

Batei Rand is accustomed to lamps. On Erev Shabbos and on Yamim Tovim when Yizkor is said, the shul is brightly lit with light that adds *kedushah* to its *kedushah* and antiquated character to its already antiquated character, until it seems that no shul in the entire world can compare to the shul in Batei Rand, with its lamps and eternal flames.

Every Erev Shabbos, Reb Shmuel Shotland (on the facing page), one of the holy people of the neighborhood, a scion of its forefathers, pours clear olive oil into fourteen glasses. A special copper plate hanging from the ceiling holds them, with a metal chain created especially for this purpose.

Great secrets hide in the way the menorah hangs, in the shape it was made and the number of its lamps. The Menorah in the Beis HaMikdash was taken by the Romans; the menorah in Batei Rand still stands as a remembrance. In the picture on this page stands Reb Shmuel's brother, Reb Aharon Dov Shotland, who, similar to the Kohen, is *"meitiv es haneiros"* — preparing the lamps.

בזכותו של בר-יוחאי

IN THE MERIT OF BAR YOCHAI

The thirty-third day of the Omer is a great day for the residents of Batei Rand. On this night, the *yahrtzeit* of Rabbi Shimon Bar Yochai, the Chassidim cancel their regular learning schedules and come to daven the early Maariv in the bustling shul.

As soon as the *shaliach tzibbur* finishes, everyone makes his way to the lamps hanging from the dome of the shul and lights an oil or wax candle in honor of the *Tanna HaEloki*. This is a great merit and *segulah* for success and all things good.

When they finish lighting the candles, the *shamash* auctions off the honor of lighting the grand *hadlakah* to the highest bidder.

*Chazakah*s are also involved, but the point is neither the auction or *chazakah*. Rather, it's the fact that when the residents of the neighborhood go out (in the picture on the facing page) to the shul courtyard with light in their eyes and delight on their faces, with a fiery torch leading them and the words "*Bar Yochai, nimshachta ashrecha*" in their mouths, no other purity, joy, or pleasure in the world can compare.

במלחמת אש-דת
Fiery Religious Battles

In Meah Shearim, there are some nights during which one can't catch any sleep until the very early morning. Even *Gedolei Olam*, such as Rabbeinu Yosef Shalom Elyashiv *zt"l* and the Slonimer Rebbe *yibadel l'chaim aruchim,* who live nearby, must listen to the sounds emanating from the *Simchos Beis HaShoeivah* on Sukkos and the dancing in honor of Rabbi Shimon Bar Yochai on the thirty-third night of the Omer.

On this night of splendor and glory, the venerated Rebbe will ignite the fire on the end of a pole, wrapped with absorbent material and immersed in olive oil, prepared specially for him.

When the *hadlakah* is ready, a *gabbai* auctions off the honor of purchasing the *hadlakah* for the Rebbe for a large sum, usually pledged by someone from overseas whose generosity supports the Chassidus. The orchestra then begins to play a song in honor of the *Tanna HaEloki* and all of Meah Shearim lights up in flames.

An authentic *hadlakah* ceremony lifts up the soul. When his legs become too heavy to continue dancing with such saintly passion, the Rebbe sits in front of the burning fire, his face aglow from the holy flames. The holy fire reflected in their Rebbe's countenance is a feast for the eyes of his Chassidim — until the tired *upsherin* boys remind them, "Tatty, tomorrow we need to go to Meron."

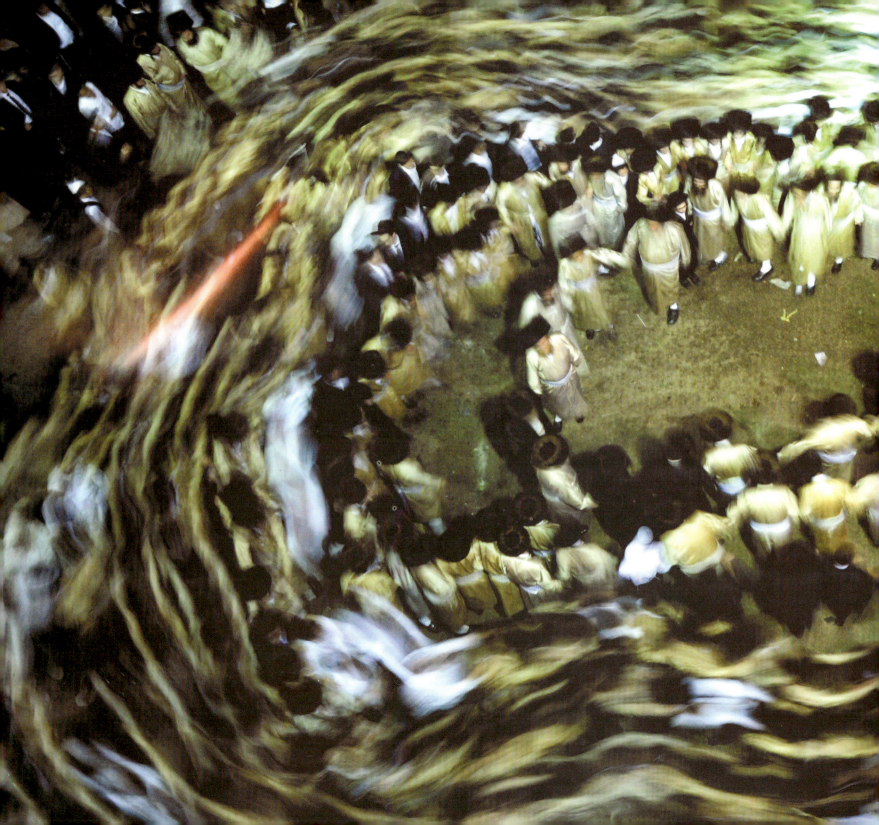

"
A real Hachnasas Sefer Torah event is the peak of excitement for the Yerushalmi child. With a burning torch in his hand, he walks alongside a rope stretched from the *chuppah* to the music car leading the way. He is entirely captivated by the joyfulness of Torah!

("With Music and Dancing," page 246)

Chapter Seven
The Month of Sivan

וקצרתם את קצירה

Reaping the Harvest

Yerushalmis love the days between Lag Ba'Omer and Shavuos, when the sages and elders harvest wheat for the *matzos mitzvah* they will eat in a little less than a year.

The emotional and physical energy the Yerushalmis invest into this labor is entirely *l'shem mitzvah*, to fulfill the mitzvah of *u'shmartem es hamatzos*. This mitzvah comes with a high price and much physical effort. The Yerushalmis don't use combines, tractors, or any other harvesting machine that would reduce the energy needed for the job; they use an old-fashioned scythe to harvest the stalks just as it was done throughout the years.

On the side of the field, sheaths of wheat wait for the long, tiring journey back to the storage room in Meah Shearim, where the wheat is protected from dampness, which could render it *chametz*. The stalks will be threshed and winnowed; when clean of chaff, the kernels will be ground in a hand-mill into the flour that the Yerushalmis will then use to make their matzos. That is the final step of the process that begins during *Sefiras Haomer* and ends on Erev Pesach.

When he finally stands next to his two kilograms of matzos, the Yerushalmi's face radiates with joy in performing this immense mitzvah. The thrill of winning a ten million-dollar lottery doesn't even come close.

בתופים ובמחולות
With Music and Dancing

On Erev Shavuos, Yerushalmi children go outside and walk in a procession holding small Sifrei Torah, and just like the adults in a Hachnasas Sefer Torah procession, they make their way down the street with a *chuppah* canopy over their heads. A real Hachnasas Sefer Torah event is the peak of excitement for the Yerushalmi child. With a burning torch in his hand, he walks alongside a rope stretched from the *chuppah* to the music car leading the way. He is entirely captivated by the joyfulness of Torah! When they reach the shul, he receives candies, to remind him of the sweetness of Torah.

The procession is headed by the "Auto-Music" — the music car with glittering, colored lights and loudspeakers that broadcast the songs in honor of Torah. One such car in the Yishuv Hayashan was driven by a *"chevraman"* named Efraim Weberman, an expert at organizing Hachnasos Sifrei Torah. Children would merrily trail behind his music car and from their high porches, mothers would watch their children dance in honor of the Torah.

The *minhag* of simulating a Hachnasas Sefer Torah on Erev Shavous is a new one; it was only just recently instituted by the Yerushalmi *chadorim*. It's a beautiful *minhag* with the power to implant *ahavas haTorah* in young and tender hearts. Perhaps *chadorim* outside the Yishuv should adopt it as well — as it says, *"mikol m'lamdai hiskalti."*

חגיגה אצל רֶבֶּ'ה מוֹישֶׁה

Festive with Rebbe Moishe

One of the more special experiences in the life of Yerushalmi *cheder* children is a Hachnasas Sefer Torah. The children are among the first to arrive at wherever the procession starts.

The organizer distributes torches to the children (replaced in recent years with the safer LED torches) and arranges them in two long rows, with ropes separating them to keep the children perfectly aligned. The children parade behind the *chuppah* covering the rabbanim, dignitaries, and donors, who dance with the Torah as it makes its way to the shul.

Two *melamdim* from "Shomrei Hachomos" can be seen in these pictures: Rebbe Klein, the second-grade teacher, and Rebbe

Hershkowitz, who teaches preschool. Rebbe Hershkowitz is an educator par excellence, so I'd like to discuss him a bit more.

Rebbe Moshe Hershkowitz is undoubtedly the most senior educator of this generation. Beginning at a young age, his shoulders have carried the weight of preschool children. His students are two-and-a-half-year-old boys, but he has no complaints. Others may look down on his profession, but the way Rebbe Hershkowitz perceives it, there's nothing more significant that he could possibly be doing. With compassion and love, he is the very first teacher to introduce his students to the *noam ol Torah* (even if the Torah is on a level more suitable for preschool children).

Whether in the rainy season or in the sun, year after year, generation after generation, Reb Moshe Hershkowitz looks after little children. He is now teaching the great-grandchildren of students who were in his class at the beginning of his career — a career that he would never exchange for any other profession in the world.

If only there were more *mechanchim* like him!

התנועה הירוקה
The Green Movement

Yerushalmi children are devoted to the *minhag* of hanging greenery in their homes and shuls in honor of Shavuos. All vegetation is suitable: large and small, green and pink, this type or that — as long as it's pleasing to the eye and contributes to the ambiance of Shavuos. Although this Yom Tov is not granted external mitzvos like a sukkah or matzah, it is adorned by this *minhag* especially beloved by the Yerushalmi children.

During the *shloshes y'mei hagbalah*, they go to the fields and orchards right after school. With alacrity, they pick and pluck all accessible greenery, put them in their sacks, and distribute them among any private or communal areas they pass on their way.

שירת העשבים

The Song of the Plants

Before Shavuos arrives, the walls and ceilings of shul will be covered with refreshing greenery. All the boys enlist in this mission, and woe unto the adult who dares try his hand at this task reserved by the children for themselves.

If Erev Sukkos is the festival of the adults who, with deep concentration, stand on street corners checking *lulavim*, *hadassim*, and *aravos*, then Shavuos is the festival of the children who stand on the same street corners and check the cypress, the eucalyptus, and the pine trees with the same concentration.

The *sefer Birkei Yosef* (494:6) alludes to the fact that the placing of greenery is a custom for children. It states, "They go up on the roof of their shul and scatter roses and apples. They gather them and say, 'Just as I am gathering the roses and apples, so too should the *bnei ha'umos* be plucked from amongst us.'"

בהיכלם של 'פרושים'
In the Perushim Shul

The old *beis midrash* in Batei Ungarin echoed the glory of the past. The *beis midrash* was very tall and its walls bore decorations that had faded over the years. Its benches were heavy and an old kerosene stove was set in its western corner. Its facade commemorated the walls of Yerushalayim. At first it was built as a shul for the Perushim community, parallel to the Chasam Sofer-Chassidish shul located nearby. But over the years, the *chaburos* of Yeshivas Hamasmidim that had started within its walls spread to additional places.

When I was a child, this is where my morning started. The shul was host to the "Chevras Tefillah," with a *mashgiach* supervising the boys' Shacharis davening in "Shomrei Hachomos." Woe to the one who didn't daven properly! This is where I spent my evenings as well. Every day after *cheder*, there was a *chevrah* here — a "*chevras limud*" with contests and prizes.

On Erev Chag Matan Torah, the children decorated the shul with fresh greenery that that they picked from the gardens of Batei Ungarin. They strung ropes from west to east and from north to south, with the flowers, leaves, and weeds draped over them. Cheerful and energetic children did this job, without the slightest thought of payment, as an expression of joy for the mitzvah and enthusiasm for Shavuos's arrival. The boy on the ladder is from the Schlesinger family: working together with his friend, he's decorating the *mikdash me'at* in preparation for the grand day on which the Torah was given.

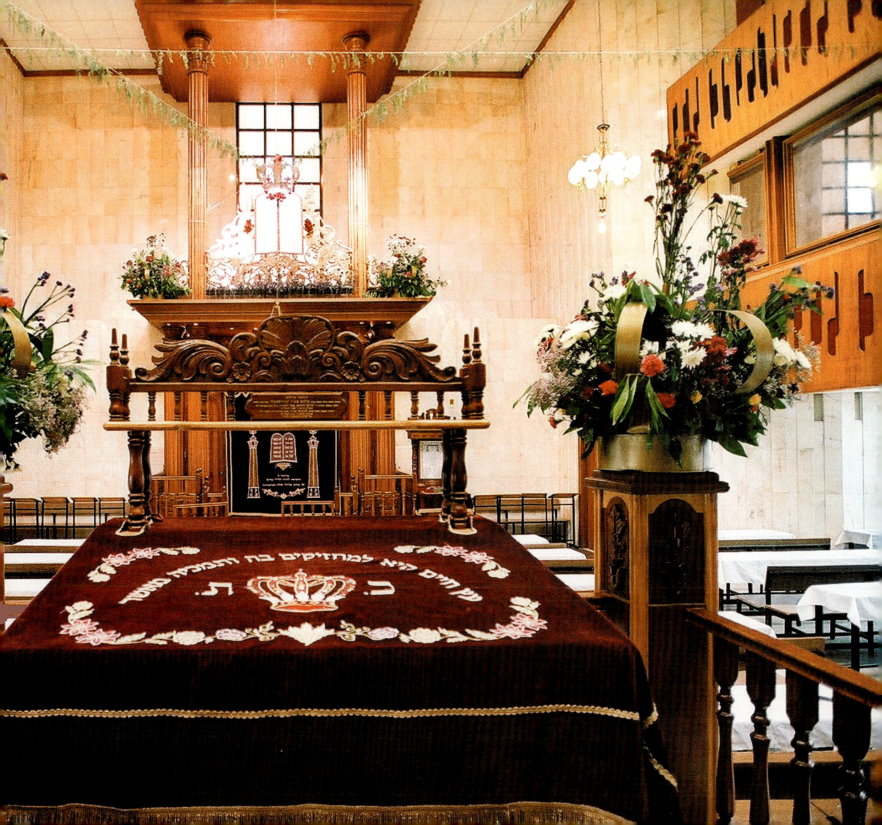

"

They read Eichah from small books, aided by the weak, flickering flames of the wax candles in their hands, providing minimal light. If wax drips and burns their hands, they aren't concerned: the pain of the *churban* hurts more than all the burns in the world.

("Mourning Yerushalayim," page 260)

Chapter Eight
Exile and Consolation

אֲבֵלֵי צִיּוֹן וִירוּשָׁלַיִם
Mourning Yerushalayim

There is no other time and place where the *churban* is mourned as on Tishah B'Av night in the Yishuv Hayashan. The shuls and *batei midrashim* are darkened, their lights turned off, fulfilling the words of *Megillas Eichah*, "*Osi nahag vayolach, choshech v'lo ohr.*" The Yerushalayim elders sit on the ground with distraught hearts, per Yirmeyah's lamentation, "*Yeishvu la'aretz yidmu, ziknei vas Tzion.*"

They read *Eichah* from small books, aided by the weak, flickering flames of the wax candles in their hands, providing minimal light. If wax drips and burns their hands, they aren't concerned: the pain of the *churban* hurts more than all the burns in the world.

The elders sit in the valley of tears and ask in a bitter voice: *Ad anah b'chiyah b'Tzion u'mispeid bi-Yerushalayim?*

After many hours of heartbreaking *kinos*, a sliver of hope and encouragement spreads through their hearts upon the voice of the *chazzan* calling out the concluding *pasuk* of *Megillas Eichah*:

Hashiveinu Hashem Eilecha v'nashuvah, chadesh yameinu k'kedem....

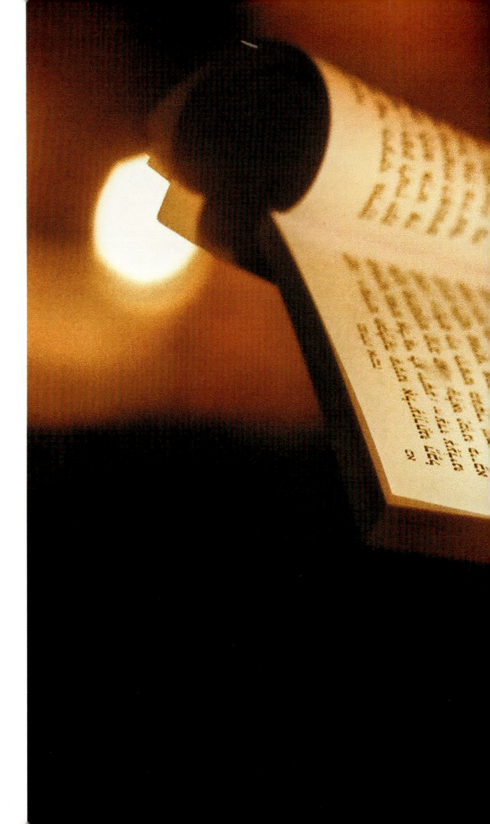

כאילו נחרב בימיו

Feeling the Destruction

The gloom felt during *Bein Hametzarim*, when Am Yisrael cries for the *churban* of the Beis HaMikdash, is felt even stronger in Yerushalayim, which is so close to the site of the destruction. The Makom HaMikdash and Hashem's city standing in spiritual desolation is like a barren woman without children.

In Yerushalayim, the mourning customs are stringently followed. There are no special "Nine-Days Menus"; Yerushalmis have no need to fill themselves with imitation meat recipes just so that, *chalilah*, their stomachs won't growl and they won't think of the *churban*.

In Yerushalayim, there are no *heterim* for listening to music during the Nine Days. There are no a capella and choral music. There is *aveilus* — straightforward *aveilus*, with no elusions or delusions.

There are *minhagim* in Yerushalayim that commemorate the *churban* during the entire year, such as no musical instruments at weddings; this is all the more pertinent during the Nine Days. The Yerushalmis make sure to feel the *churban* on every single one of these days. All around, you see old people who've been trained since babyhood not to laugh during the Nine Days, not to rejoice, and not to indulge in idle chatter. They move about with despondent faces, with expressions of gravity and worry, and don't allow their minds to stray from thinking about the *churban*. Remaining focused, they adhere to our Sages' words, *"Kol dor shelo nivneh Beis HaMikdash b'yamav, k'ilu nechrav b'yamav."*

זִקְנֵי בַת צִיּוֹן

The Rebbe's Prayer

As the sadness deepens, mischievous children go up to the *ezras nashim* and playfully throw down bags of *"bobkes"* — pine cones — on the mourners' heads. Those who are davening get angry, but the children smile, happy that they managed to diminish the mourning to some extent.

The only source found for this prank is in the anecdote that Chassidim relate about Rebbe Yisrael of Ruzhin *zy"a*. One Tishah B'Av he entered the shul and fell victim to a prank. Some young Chassidim had climbed up to the *ezras nashim* and, using ropes attached to a wooden board placed on the floor of the shul, managed to hoist up everyone who entered the *beis midrash*. The Rebbe entered the shul unnoticed by the Chassidim, and he too was lifted and swung around!

When the young Chassidim realized that it was none other than the Rebbe they had caught in their net, they panicked and fled, leaving the Rebbe suspended between Heaven and earth. Rebbe Yisrael lifted his eyes and proclaimed, "*Ribon HaOlamim*, see your beloved, suffering children who don't know how to cope with this 'Yom Tov.' Please, take it from us and bring us Mashiach Tzidkeinu."

יֵשְׁבוּ לָאָרֶץ יִדְּמוּ

Grief and Sorrow

Awareness of the *churban* of Yerushalayim is transmitted from father to son; even small children can sense the somber atmosphere by being taught to decrease their consumption of sweets during these days.

Children sit on the floor with their fathers and read *Megillas Eichah* by the light of a candle, although they can't yet appreciate the value of *Zevul Beis Mikdasheinu*.

Here, a father and son from Toldos Aharon sit together on the floor of Yeshuos Yaakov, and mourn the *churban*. The father works for the *Chevrah Kaddisha*. He encounters grief and sorrow every day of the year. Yet even so, on the night of Tishah B'Av, grief and sorrow are etched in his face far more than when he works.

Although he knows that when the Beis HaMikdash is rebuilt the dead will stand again, thus leaving him with no source of income, he nevertheless longs for the *Geulah* with all of his heart; his *parnasah* is a minute sacrifice for such a monumental goal.

> There is no time purer than the minutes after the Minchah of Erev Yom Kippur that includes a lengthy *viduy*. After this Minchah, the pure-minded people walk to their homes to eat the *seudah* and to prepare for the great day. The *ba'alei nefesh* feel the special purity that descends on the world and fills the air. They're like angels, without even the slightest vestige of a fleeting thought of sin.

("Pure by Our Father in Heaven," page 289)

Chapter Nine

The Days of Awe

שְׁטֵייט אוּף צוּ סְלִיחֶעס
Get Up for Selichos

A white tallis seems to spread out over the alleys of Meah Shearim at *chatzos* of Motza'ei Shabbos, the first night of Selichos for the Ashkenazim. At this untainted hour, the old and young of Meah Shearim make their way to the neighborhood shuls, each individual to the shul that davens in his particular *nusach* — a Litvak to a *nusach* Ashkenaz shul, a Chassid to a shul of Chassidim, and even a small shul for Sephardim, deep inside the *shuk* and across from the Toldos Avraham Yitzchak shul. Whichever shul, whatever *nusach*, all share a feeling of gravity as they hold their Selichos book with trembling hands.

On the other side of the alley, the righteous Yerushalmi women climb the steps to the *ezras nashim*. They too wake up early every morning to say Selichos. They cry out to Hashem and plead on behalf of their children and the nation that the year, with its many curses, comes to an end and a year of blessing begins. They ask the Compassionate Forgiver to decree a year of redemption for His people.

At the designated time, the sounds of Selichos are heard. In the old Chabad Shul on Ba'al Hatanya Street, enthusiastic Chassidim conclude their appeal for forgiveness with a Chassidish dance, accompanied by an old Chassidish *niggun* woven from words of the Selichos:

רַחֲמָנָא דְעָנֵי לַעֲנִיֵּי עֲנֵינָן.
רַחֲמָנָא דְעָנֵי לִתְבִירֵי לִבָּא עֲנֵינָן.

התרת נדרים

ANULLING VOWS

The locals refer to this shul as *"Di Hungarishe Shul"* — the Hungarian Shul. Why is the shul named after the historic Kingdom of Hungary? Did Emperor Franz Joseph, who was greatly admired by the Jews of the kingdom, donate money for the shul's construction? Actually, the only connection between Franz Joseph and the shul is that his subjects built it when they moved to Yerushalayim. Since its founders were Hungarian immigrants, the shul will forever be known as the Hungarian Shul.

The thick walls of the shul, founded by Rav Dovid Weber *zt"l*, are saturated with layers of *kedushah* that have amassed from a hundred years of davening and Torah learning. Its benches are timeworn and its dozen windows overlook the courtyard of the *mikveh* on the east and the Talmud Torah on the west. It's a long and narrow shul, but despite its simplicity, it expresses grandeur of old.

The shul is inscribed in my head and on my heart. On Friday nights during the rainy season, the vapor rising from cups of scalding tea poured from a samovar standing near the shul's entrance, permeated the *beis midrash*. Melodious sounds of learning spread throughout the *beis midrash*, accompanied by incomparable sweetness.

Above all, the shul's uniqueness is expressed during the Tishrei Yamim Tovim. On Hoshana Rabbah night, *Sefer Devarim* is read from an old Sefer Torah by a few *ba'alei keriah* who switch off with one another in the middle. Everybody dons a white *kittel* because this is, on a smaller scale, a day of judgment. On Yom Kippur, the *beis midrash* is ablaze from the heat of the candles burning within a copper box, placed on the windowsill in the west of the shul. Another interesting Tishrei fact: on Sukkos 1986, I was redeemed in the shul's sukkah for five *selaim*.

In this picture, the shul's *mispalelim* are davening on the morning of Erev Rosh Hashanah as they annul every vow, oath, and promise. Those waiting for *hataras nedarim* include Torah giants, such as Rav Levi Rabinowitz and Rav Leibish Deutsch. They share the *hataras nedarim* area with a young *bachur* named Gruber, an exceptional *avreich* today. The middle *dayan* whose back is towards the camera is Rav Velvel Gutfarb, a legendary resident of the neighborhood.

זמן כפרה
Time for *Kapparah*

During the early morning hours of Erev Yom Kippur, the lot by the slaughterhouse in the Meah Shearim *shuk* is a hullabaloo of poultry cackles and human cries, blending together in one holy cacophony. Yoelish, the slaughterhouse jack-of-all-trades, walks around with enthusiastic energy. His beard, normally black, is white from all the feathers that are stuck to it, and his pants and vest are soiled from the birds of atonement. Yoelish honors his clients with a good, healthy rooster, the best of the best, a praiseworthy *kapparah*. Cackling, atoning roosters and people in search of atonement surround him. This is the eve of the holy day, a time of atonement for one and all.

מָצָאתִי כֹפֶר

I Have Found Atonement

The days between Rosh Hashanah and Yom Kippur is the time for swirling a rooster around one's head for a *kapparah, temurah,* and *chalifah* — a rooster for each person.

Those who are the most *mehader* with *kapparos* save this ceremony for the last third of the night before Yom Kippur, a time during which a thread of *chesed* is extended over the entire world.

"*B'nei adam yoshvei choshech v'tzalmaves*" is murmured by those seeking atonement. And after they finish with "*peda'eihu meiredes shachas matzasi chofer,*" they swing the rooster around their heads, rendering it the *kapparah, temurah,* and *chalifah* for their sins and iniquities.

Pictured is Rav Yeshayah Deutsch *zt"l*, carrying his *kapparah* from the slaughterhouse.

לפני השם תטהרו
Cleansed before Hashem

Yerushalmi elders are characterized by equanimity. They have only one way of serving Hashem and interacting with people. During times of stress or times of serenity, in times of anger and times of joy, they radiate poise and self-control, never getting agitated or nervous. Yerushalmis can dance with a *chosson* and *kallah* with the same expressionless face they wear when being *melaveh* the dead.

The same is true of their *avodas Hashem*. The elders of the Yishuv Hayashan who are not part of the Chassidish community daven the *tefillah* of Erev Yom Kippur exactly the same way they would daven Minchah on a grey day in Teves. (Not that their Minchah on a grey day in Teves is heartless and detached!) Whether at a time of sublime exaltedness or a time of routine, they concentrate on the words, and recognize and appreciate before Whom they stand.

Here, two Yerushalmi elders, Rav Dovid Cheshin and his friend, sit in Yeshuos Yaakov on Erev Yom Kippur, a few hours before the start of the day of forgiveness, sharing ideas about the essence of the day. They know that throughout the year every one of their deeds was guided by the *Shulchan Aruch*. They never missed a *zeman tefillah*, didn't cause harm to anyone, and didn't insult anybody. They designated time to learn Torah and were friendly and gracious to everybody they met. And if there is some slight blemish? They are aware of what it is and will concentrate on it while they daven; after all, *"ki bayom hazeh y'chaper aleichem l'taher eschem mikol chatoseichem."*

והוא רחום יכפר

THE MERCIFUL ONE FORGIVES

When *malkos* are given, the individual being lashed prostrates himself on a cloth, separating him from the ground. He faces southward and strikes his chest with his right hand. A strap of leather is used for the thirty-nine lashes, divided between the right side, the left side, and the middle of the back.

During the lashing, the ones giving and receiving the lashes repeat the *pasuk* "*V'Hu rachum y'chaper avon*" until all the lashes are meted out. The one who was lashed gets up with the knowledge that if he had sinned during the year, he is now pardoned and exonerated. He is a new creature, a blank sheet of paper that can now be filled with mitzvos and *ma'asim tovim*.

Of course, this isn't a real beating with backbreaking lashes that would call for police intervention. These are gentle strokes from a leather strap that are hardly felt at all, just a commemoration of the *malkos* meted out in the times of the Sanhedrin. If a person feels he deserves lashes, he imagines actually receiving them, which then prompts him to do *teshuvah shleimah*.

בקדושה ובטהרה

Revealed and Hidden

Two giants glorified the *Mizrach* of the Toldos Avraham Yitzchak Chassidus, which splintered off from Toldos Aharon and was lead by the Admor, whose heart blazed with a passion smelted from the fire of Vishnitz and the contemplation of Shomrei Emunim. One of these magnificent people was famed for his familiarity with *Toras Haniglah* and the other for his expertise in *Toras Hanistar*. Rav Meir Bransdorfer was a *posek hador*; Rav Daniel Frisch was the Rosh Yeshiva of the *kabbalistic* Sha'ar HaShamayim Yeshiva.

What was the source of this relationship between a halachic master and a mystic? In this case, *yir'as Shamayim* and Chassidus united them as soul friends — one the halachic support for the masses in need of a *psak*, and one the address for the *y'chidei segulah* who delved into the writings of *sod*. Rav Meir and Rav Daniel brought glory to Batei Ungarin and davened in Toldos Aharon, in the shadow of the Admor, the Divrei Emunah zt"l. At the end of their lives, when the Chassidus split, both relocated to the *beis midrash* of Toldos Avraham Yitzchak in Meah Shearim.

The picture on the far left depicts the *mekubal*, Rav Daniel Frisch zt"l. The one on the right shows Rav Meir Bransdorfer zt"l (L) with Rav Yaakov Tzvi Samet *yibadel l'chaim* (R) walking through the arched gate of Batei Neitin following the *seudah hamafsekes*, on their way to the Meah Shearim *shuk*. Their faces express fear of the approaching judgment, their very walk conveys the purity of their hearts, while their lips whisper a prayer — *Ki kadosh hayom La'Adoneinu*.

דומים למלאכים
Like Angels

Two personalities walk on the main street of Meah Shearim, brought together by happenstance because there is no correlation between the two of them.

The one on the left is Rav Avraham Rotman *zt"l*, an outstanding figure from Batei Neitin, operator of a *gemach* that lends out tefillin and of a long-forgotten organization called "Hasa'ad HaRuchani." Rav Rotman is a family man, whose many descendants glorify his table — *kish'silei zeisim saviv l'shulchanecha*.

Rav Baruch Yosef Levi *zt"l* is the other person in the picture. He was a childless man who chose Torah as his loyal friend and partner. He immigrated from America some time in the distant past. Since then, his world was limited to the narrow room in Beis Yisrael where he took a quick nap during the night, and the Chabad Shul in Meah Shearim, where his head was bent over the worn Gemaras that he finished one after another. He was a consummate *masmid* with unparalleled *hasmadah*, but he thought nothing of himself.

From his little room, he walked to his place of study holding a clattering tzedakah box, collecting for the poor and lonely people whose souls were revived with warm, nourishing soup at Kollel Chabad's soup kitchen. He too, without a wife or relative, ate there.

The locked Deshen restaurant, operated by Rav Shlomo Lustig *zt"l*, can be seen on the right; on the left is a bicycle, a vehicle which has no use on the eve of this holy day. In the middle walk two Jews preparing themselves for the awesome day about which it is said, *"V'chol adam lo yihiyeh b'ohel moed bevo'o l'chaper bakodesh ad tzeiso."*

לפני מי אתם מיטהרין
Pure by Our Father in Heaven

There is no time purer than the minutes after the Minchah of Erev Yom Kippur that includes a lengthy *viduy*. After this Minchah, the pure-minded people walk to their homes to eat the *seudah* and to prepare for the great day. The *ba'alei nefesh* feel the special purity that descends on the world and fills the air. They're like angels, without even the slightest vestige of a fleeting thought of sin.

In the picture on the right is Rav Meir Blau, son of Rav Uri Blau, the head *Kanai* in the generation after his father, Rav Amram Blau. Rav Meir integrates the *kanaus* of his father with the relative openness of the *Masmidim*. On Lag Ba'Omer, Rav Meir stands, together with the orchestra, on the platform in Meron, singing with passionate *kavanah* and a dry throat to groups of humanity that are swept away with *dveikus* and sacred passion:

אמר רבי עקיבא:
אשריכם ישראל,
לפני מי אתם מיטהרין ומי מטהר אתכם?
אביכם שבשמים!
מה מקווה מטהר את הטמאים –
אף הקדוש ברוך הוא מטהר את ישראל.

תפילה זכה

TEFILLAH ZAKAH

One of the oldest Yerushalmis leaves early to Toldos Aharon in order to say *Tefillah Zakah* slowly and carefully. He knows not how many more Yom Kippurs his Creator will grant him. He rejoices in meriting to begin a new year and approach another Yom Kippur. May his Creator continue granting him lengthy days and years until *bi'as goel tzedek*.

די אַלטע קאַרלינער׳ס
The Old Karliners

Pinsk-Karlin is a golden link in the generational chain of Chassidus. This Chassidish court dedicates itself to *avodas Elokim* with *perishus*, passion, and emotion, like all early Yerushalmi Chassidish dynasties.

They don't budge even a hairsbreadth from the conduct of the early Chassidim. They even refer to themselves as *"Di Alte Karliners"* — the Old Karliners, testifying to their adherence to the ways of old. Even though their ranks are bursting with young Chassidim who are like new jugs, full and overflowing with the fragrance and spirit of old, they still use this name.

The community's first leader was Admor Aharon HaKohen Rosenfeld *zt"l*, who led the young-old Chassidim in a unique manner that incorporated both *ahavah* and *yirah*.

After his passing, his oldest son, Rav Aryeh Kohen Rosenfeld, took over his father's throne. Like his father, he didn't budge from the *minhagim* of the Yerushalmi Chassidim: he wore a gold-striped caftan, copied the form and speech of the elders, and instilled the young among his Chassidim with the fiery blaze of pure Chassidus.

Here he sits, wrapped in a white caftan, during an awe-inspiring Chassidish gathering held on the eve of Yom Kippur. Surrounding him, like Shlomo Hamelech's sixty strong warriors, are the elders of the Chassidus, including his Rosh Yeshiva, Rav Yisrael Grossman *zt"l*, one of the immense giants of *Yerushalayim shel Maalah*. In front of him sit his young Chassidim. They sing the melodies of the holy day, meditating on complete *teshuvah*, as is appropriate for the rapidly approaching day.

כשם שאני רוקד

THE END OF THE DAY

If the stones of the Chassidish shul in Batei Ungarin could speak, they would tell tales of giants who concealed their greatness and Torah genius, never using their Torah as a tool for practical gain. They would speak about pure and honest Yerushalmis who are removed from any concept of honor and respect in their daily schedule, who are composed and complacent about material concerns, but zealous and emotional when it comes to spiritual matters.

On the wall next to the shul, at the feet of the Kiddush Levanah sign, the pasted *pashkevil* notices of the Yishuv announce that So-and-so ascended to the *Yeshivah shel Maalah*, that graves are being desecrated somewhere, thus warranting a protest, and that a closeout sale at an ancient *sefarim* store is offering dusty wares for just a few pennies.

On the facing page is Rav Mordechai Sheinberger following the *avodah* of the awesome day, speaking with a distinguished neighbor, Rav Dovid Weider. On the left is Rav Rotman *zt"l*, being *mekadesh* the *levanah* on Motza'ei Yom Kippur.

Nearby is the sukkah that a neighbor leaves standing from Sukkos to Sukkos, a symbol of his love for the mitzvah.

"
Some children in the Yishuv Hayashan are experts at *koishiklach*, the braided holders made of *lulav* branches that hold the *arba minim* together. A week before Sukkos, these children wander around the *shuk* trying to sell their *koishiklach*, two for a shekel. If they return home with seven shekels in their pocket, they couldn't be happier.

("The Art of *Koishiklach*," page 311)

Chapter Ten
Sukkos

אַ סוּכָּהלֶ'ה אַ קְלֵיינֶע
A Temporary Dwelling

The children of the Yishuv Hayashan love the mitzvah of sukkah. Their faces sparkle as they help their fathers build. Like experienced carpenters, they saw and drill, sort *"keines"* and drag *"parvanes"* (boards).

Anywhere else, these children would have been rebuked long ago. How can they handle a saw at this age — and risk cutting off their fingers?! But in Yerushalayim, fathers trust their children to be cautious, are confident in their maturity and expertise, and are secure in the knowledge that *"shomer mitzvah lo yeida davar ra."*

Already two weeks before the Yom Tov arrives, the children stroll among the sukkahs, satisfied with the labor of their hands, comparing sukkahs, measuring them and copying ideas. There is nothing like the joy of a Yerushalmi child seeing his father's sukkah, which he helped build, standing strong. It's a fulfillment of *"Amaleinu — eilu habanim."* Though this sentence really refers to Pesach, it's appropriate for Sukkos as well, which is preceded by the toil of the Yerushalmi children constructing worthy sukkahs.

Sukkos in Meah Shearim draws many curious tourists interested in viewing this picturesque neighborhood, its courtyards jam-packed with wooden sukkahs. There is a complicated relationship between the residents and tourists: sometimes the encounter can be suspicious and distrustful, and at other times, particularly during solitary encounters, warm and welcoming. People don't appreciate being studied like a museum exhibit or like monkeys in the zoo. In this regard, the inhabitants of Meah Shearim and Batei Ungarin differ from the residents of the "Shtetlach," who warmly and graciously greet the tourists.

האמן מההכניסה לשוק
The Artist at the Entrance to the Shuk

A skeletal, steep staircase led to Reb Yaakov Weisberg's magical home at the entrance to the Meah Shearim *shuk*.

Reb Yaakov Weisberg lived here his entire life, crafting and creating. He was an autodidact, an artist who learned everything on his own, without teacher and training. His creations could be included among those of the greatest artists in the world, but if you knew Weisberg, you understood why his art never crossed the threshold of international exhibitions, why he didn't pursue distinguished prizes, and why he didn't sell his creations for fees that would have kept him and his progeny fed for generations. Nor did he merit widespread recognition in the *chareidi* world, because this type of recognition and admiration is reserved for Torah giants. Even so, Weisberg was completely satisfied with his small, charming G-dly portion and rejoiced in his pure, simple creations.

He never sought fame or prominence. In the morning, he'd go to shul with a threadbare tefillin bag that he had artistically decorated. After davening, he returned to his room to paint, build, and document Jewish life in *Yerushalayim shel Maalah* and forgotten European villages with an artist's hand and a sensitive soul. Underneath his home, military parades marked the day that the State was established and noisy demonstrations protested the State's transgressions, but he was undisturbed. He focused on his art, which wasn't influenced by time or era, but infused with Yerushalmi innocence and charm.

Weisberg made all kinds of creations: miniature models of ancient shuls, a large wall embellished with an almost-exact reproduction of the Kosel; the entire *Shir Hashirim* written on the peel of an egg, and a Me'aras Hamachpelah so lifelike that if you'd close your eyes, you'd hear the prayers within and feel the sanctity of the Avos. His works were conservative but creative; related to Torah sources but aided by techniques of modern art. He painted the walls and ceilings of most shuls in the area, and if he wasn't the one who painted them, he at least added some of his own charm when restoring the works of earlier Yerushalmi painters. Thousands of *Shivisi Hashem L'negdi Samid* signs created by his artistic hands were scattered among many shuls in Yerushalayim, before the advent of rapid printing and graphic effects.

On Sukkos, Reb Yaakov opened the door of his home to the masses. There were no family visits in his sukkah, because the grandfather-artist was busy greeting the public. Night after night, he gave lectures to groups and explained to individuals for the millionth time about the exact material he used to create the miniature model of the Mishkan, and the precise scale used for his model of the Beis HaMikdash. He shared the concepts behind his artwork with infinite patience and graciousness.

I saw him for the last time on Rosh Hashanah of 2017. He was at the peak of old age at 96. He had to stop his artwork because of shaky hands, but still enjoyed his life's handiwork. On the second day of Yom Tov, after davening and the last *tekios*, he invited me into his home to see his works of art. Although I grew up very familiar with his art, I happily acquiesced. Some things you can see a thousand times yet still discover new angles and more hidden ideas — and if a 96-year-old artist lives and breathes his work at this age and finds nourishment from it, I have a lot to learn from him.

Reb Yaakov was wearing a faded white *kittel* when he welcomed me into his home. His eyes shone when he showed me the animals symbolizing the *shivtei Yisrael*, the waterfalls in his miniature model zoo, the reliefs of the eagle, leopard, deer, and lion from the Mishnah of Rabbi Yehudah ben Teimah, and his exact replica of the Hungarishe Shul in Meah Shearim. His works crossed continents: Reb Yaakov proudly showed me his reproduction of the World Headquarters of Chabad in Crown Heights that he created with tens of thousands of small matches.

Reb Weisberg was the last of the authentic Meah Shearim residents, a vestige of a generation that lived there before it was conquered by notices, *pashkevils*, and the atmosphere created by the recently arrived extremists. He didn't gain international recognition, but in those few minutes when I made my last visit to his small, dilapidated, magnificent, and artistic home, I felt that Reb Yaakov would feel more gratified by a Jew impressed with his work than he would from any number of international prestigious prizes.

I am almost certain that right now, up above, he is busy making a miniature replica of Gan Eden.

שואלין ודורשין
Thirty Days Before

Those meticulous in mitzvos begin delving into the *kashrus* of *lulavim* and *esrogim* thirty days before the Yom Tov begins. In other parts of the Jewish world, people are busy preparing for the Yamim Noraim — cleaning the head of the fish for a *"simana tava,"* preparing spinach latkes and *"rubiya"* seeds for Rosh Hashanah, and practicing the shofar for the Yom Hadin — but in Yerushalayim they're already standing outside of the *beis hora'ah*, meticulously checking *lulavim*.

Checking a *lulav* in the Yishuv Hayashan calls for a lot of patience. Its spine must be ramrod straight and its middle leaves completely sealed. There are many additional rules regarding the *lulav*, but for now, it's not the laws of *arba minim* that interests us, but rather the special atmosphere that pervades Yerushalayim from mid-Elul.

The closer it gets to Sukkos, the more tumult there is around the *arba minim*. It becomes so busy that nary a street corner in Geulah and Meah Shearim can be seen without a thick-bearded man squinting through a magnifying glass to inspect the spine of a *lulav*, the *pitom* of an *esrog*, the tripled leaves of the hadas, or the tip of an *aravah*.

אמנות ה'קוֹישִׁיקְלַאךְ'

THE ART OF *KOISHIKLACH*

Some children in the Yishuv Hayashan are experts at *koishiklach*, the braided holders made of *lulav* branches that hold the *arba minim* together. A week before Sukkos, these children wander around the *shuk* trying to sell their *koishiklach*, two for a shekel. If they return home with seven shekels in their pocket, they couldn't be happier.

סוכה שהיא גבוהה
A Street Cat or Eisenbach

The sanctity of Batei Ungarin even reaches the street cats that pass through its alleys. These cats are unique, because as they saunter between the garbage cans and alleyways, they have the ability to appreciate their lucky fate of being placed in a location free of this world's defects. It is said that if someone would throw a stone in Batei Ungarin it would either hit a street cat or someone named Eisenbach — because there are so many Eisenbachs in the neighborhood.

Nowhere else in Yerushalayim are sukkahs constructed next to each other in such an eye-catching way as they are in the big courtyard at the center of Batei Ungarin. One needs to be trained in acrobatics in order to pass between the sukkahs — a contraction of the body as you walk sideways — to make sure not to bump the side of a sukkah and wake the sleepers from their slumber.

The residents of Batei Ungarin love their sukkahs so much that if they could, they would extend the Yom Tov by two weeks or more. Even the Yerushalmi cats can't disturb the serenity of those sleeping in their sukkahs in the *reshus harabim*.

ולקחתם לכם
Take for Yourselves

Great is the rejoicing on the morning of the first day of Sukkos when the members of the Yishuv Hayashan walk to shul like light-footed soldiers, brandishing their *lulavim* and exulting over the mitzvah with shining eyes. One hand holds a *lulav* with fragrant *hadassim* and fresh *aravos*; the other hand holds an *esrog* wrapped in *"kloshin"* — flax fibers.

The mitzvah of *lulav* unites old and young. There is no differentiating between an old man like Rav Avraham Rotman *zt"l* (picture on the facing page) from Batei Neitin, who is preparing to fulfill the mitzvah of *lulav* for the eightieth time, and a ten-year-old child who merits to fulfill the mitzvah for just his fourth or fifth time. Other than the wisdom of an older man, the old and the young are one and the same: the joy is the same joy, the purity of soul is the same purity of soul, and the spark in the eye is the same spark in the eye — whether in the clear eyes of a young boy or the eyes, dimmed by old age, of the one who blesses his great-grandchildren every Friday night, per the Yerushalmi custom.

The awe-inspiring connection between the generations in *Yerushalayim shel Maalah* is knitted out of joy for a mitzvah, desire for Torah, and the purity of mind that is found exclusively between the curved alleys of old Yerushalayim.

בצילא דמהימנותא

Under Hashem's Protection

Rav Yitzchak Nosson Kuperstock sits in his cozy sukkah learning Torah in the "Shtetlach," surrounded by a plethora of sukkah decorations made by his own hands. He was a man of light and of beauty, reflected both in his personality and his handiwork. His family says that some of the decorations were an inheritance from his parents and crafted more than 150 years ago.

Unlike the private sukkahs in the Yishuv Hayashan that are covered with decorations made by Yerushalmis and their wives, the shul's sukkahs are bedecked with ancient *parochos*. Though these *parochos* are no longer used to adorn the Aron Kodesh, it's only befitting that they be used for the mitzvah of decorating the sukkah. Indeed, there is no decoration more striking than velvet *parochos* with gold-threaded embroidery, memorializing distinguished Yerushalmis who passed on to the Next World. True, the *parochos* are worn, but the wear-and-tear for a mitzvah doesn't impact internal splendor.

In this picture, the elders of the Mazkeres neighborhood in the "Shtetlach" learn Daf Yomi after davening, surrounded by *parochos* that drape the shul's sukkah. The *Shechinah* hovers above them and envelopes them on all sides.

אורות וצללים
Lights and Shadows

The words of *"A Sukkale a Kleine,"* the ancient Yiddish song composed in Poland by Avraham Reisen, echoes through rickety sukkahs with their mismatched, moldy boards, and sheets to disguise their many holes, standing in the Batei Wittenberg plaza. Just like the words of the song, the few boards and the *schach* battle the sharp, shrill winds that whistle during the nights in the open areas. The wind penetrates the cracks, stirs the sheets, battles with the lamps, and threatens to damage and destroy. But the sukkah, the eternal Jewish sukkah, stands straight-backed, shaky but strong, persecuted but determined, almost tumbling — but never actually falling.

The sukkah on the facing page is exactly the opposite: it's made of shimmering sheets through which one can see silhouettes dancing joyfully. Another silhouette can also be seen: the shadow of a Jew sitting in his sukkah late at night on Chol HaMoed, surrounded by *Tzila Di'Mehemnusa* and learning Torah with great devotion.

Behind the sukkah boards and the gas balloons, you get a peek of Rav Mordechai Aharon Sheinberger *zt"l*, a Torah great of Batei Ungarin, who had every secret of the Torah stored in his mind for ninety-three years. Anywhere else, he would have been singled out for his greatness, but here, in the Yishuv Hayashan, diamonds of Torah and *yirah* walk like regular people, drawing no attention to themselves.

בלשון חסידים
THE WORDS OF CHASSIDIM

Rav Yosef Aharon Derenfeld was one of Batei Ungarin's very special residents. A Chabad Chassid through and through and an American by birth, he was very conspicuous in the neighborhood. Every day, he left the protective walls of Batei Ungarin on his bike. When he reached Ben Yehudah Street — geographically close by but light-years away — he stood on the sidewalk and lay tefillin on the arms and heads of lost Jewish souls.

During the Second Intifada a terrible terrorist attack occurred on that street. For a good few hours, his wife and friends worried that perhaps he was involved in the tragedy. Their fears were finally laid to rest when he pedaled back home on his bicycle, unaware of the terrorist attack and his family's worries, happy and fulfilled after another day of Chabad "*mivtzaim*" was behind him.

At the end of his life, he suffered a stroke and was hospitalized in the Neveh Simchah Nursing Home. His wife, an outstanding figure in her own right, brought him home on the Yamim Tovim and arranged for Chassidim to *farbreng* with him; after all, a *farbrengen* can accomplish things in the upper worlds that even the angel Michael cannot.

Here the Rebbe of Kuzmir, the tzaddik Rav Yehoshua (Reb Sheah) Kornblit, speaks sweet words of *aggadah* in Rav Yosef Aharon's bare-walled sukkah. Chabad Chassidim don't decorate their sukkahs because their guests are their best sukkah decorations.

Also seen in this picture is the legendary *shakdan* from the Chabad Shul in Meah Shearim, Rav Baruch Yosef ben Rav Nachum Leib HaLevi Levin *zt"l*; *yibadel l'chaim aruchim*, Rav Herschel Chanon, the shul's *gabbai*; Reb Shimshon Halevi Tas, a "man of the Kosel"; along with the profile of the one writing these lines when he was a young *bachur*.

הפרטיזן מבתי אונגרין

The Partisan from Batei Ungarin

Legends claim that Reb Aharon Yaakov Resnitz was a partisan. He lived in Batei Ungarin next to the Chassidish shul named for the Chasam Sofer. A blue number was etched in his arm and his eyes reflected a life soaked in *yissurim* and heroism. Every day, he collected tzeddakah in the Meah Shearim *shtieblach*.

Another rumor claims that the partisan didn't collect money for his own use, but distributed it all to tzedakah causes. A trustworthy witness stated that on Erev Rosh Hashanah, the partisan placed ten thousand shekels into the hand of a poor man with a big family and told him that it was for Yom Tov necessities, and then swore him to secrecy.

את משנה התורה הזאת

Hoshana Rabbah Night

After six days of rejoicing, Yerushalmis gather at shul on Hoshana Rabbah night. They dress in white, as appropriate for the day designated as the continuation of Yom Kippur, when Heavenly *"piska"* notes are sent to execute the decrees that were written on Rosh Hashanah and sealed on Yom Kippur.

On Hoshana Rabbah, *simchas Yom Tov* is diluted with fear of judgment. The drums and wind instruments from the Simchas Beis HaShoeiva no longer reverberate, but the mitzvah of *v'samachta b'chagecha* still stands. Presently, on the night when the *piska* notes are sent, everyone goes to shul to read Mishneh Torah together in honor of tomorrow's Simchas Torah.

The most expert *ba'al korei* ascends the *bimah* to read the entire *Chumash Devarim*, from its beginning until its end, starting with *"Eileh devarim"* and ending with *"l'einei kol Yisrael."* If he is elderly and cannot read the entire Chumash, a young *ba'al korei* takes over, allowing the senior *ba'al korei* to gather his strength for the concluding *parashios* of the Torah. Finally, everybody in shul exuberantly repeats after the *ba'al korei*: *Chazak, Chazak V'nischazeik!*

This Torah reading is done very quickly: everybody still needs to recite the entire *Sefer Tehillim*, eat a light meal — each person in his own sukkah — and wake up early for the lengthy Hoshana Rabbah davening, which involves many deep secrets and *segulos*. The quick *ba'al korei* finishes *Sefer Devarim* in an hour or an hour and a half, after which he's suitably rewarded with pats on his back, warm handshakes, and resounding *"yasher koach"*s.

When I was young, I used to accompany Rav Moshe Weber *zt"l* to the Mishneh Torah reading. In this picture, you can see the residents of Batei Ungarin in the Hungarishe Shul at the Mishneh Torah reading. The *ba'al korei* is Rav Menachem Mendel Meshi-Zahav, a Yerushalmi *sofer* who had an incredible ability to *lein*. From time to time, he switches off with Rav Yitzchak Eizik Stern, who walked from his home in Shikun Rabbanim to participate in this Mishneh Torah.

When the *leining* is concluded, everyone returns home in peace — but not before tasting banana liquor and some *lekach* purchased from the Brizel Bakery. The Hershler Family has a *yahrtzeit* on this date, so they invite everyone to the shul's sukkah to make a *berachah* on a piece of cake and a little cup of schnapps.

Everyone in shul graciously shares blessings for *"a gut kvittel"* — a good, sweet year — and when they leave shul, they are greeted by young boys selling bundles of fresh *aravos* which will be used during the morning davening.

הושענא רבה בכבשן הסלונימאי
Hoshana Rabbah in Fiery Slonim

A collective expression of emotions flows from the windows of the spacious *tisch* room. This is an ancient room in modern style, with walls covered in light brown wood, a tall ceiling with excellent acoustics, and dim lighting that bathes the room in an inspiring glow. At its front is a magnificent Aron Kodesh covered with a *paroches* clean of text other than the *pasuk* "*V'Hashem b'heichal kadsho hass mipanav kol ha'aretz.*"

Welcome to the passionate fire of Slonim.

The Slonim Chassidus is an island of separatism, a unique reservation that maintains a relationship of both distance and closeness with everything that happens around it. It prides itself on being an elite unit among the Chassidish fortresses, with the cultural gap between them almost too large to bridge.

This is Slonim, the senior Chassidus that can't be compared to any other Chassidish court, to the Litvish Torah world, or to any other type. Slonim is unique, radiant with its separatism and separate with its radiance.

On Hoshana Rabbah, the Chassidim join together for a special *tisch*. The Rebbe resembles a *malach*, dressed only in white. The *tisch* is similar to Neilah; it includes songs of devotion and yearning, passages from the Yamim Noraim, and the melodies and lyrics of the *sanigorian shel Yisrael*, Rav Levi Yitzchak of Berditchov *zy"a*, which address the Creator of the World with the candor of a son to his father:

"מִזְרָח דּוּ, מַעֲרָב דּוּ, דָּרוֹם דּוּ, צָפוֹן דּוּ, מַעֲלָה דּוּ, מַטָּה דּוּ, דּוּ, דּוּ, דּוּ. אַז עֶס אִיז גוּט, אִיז דָאךְ דּוּ, אַז חָלִילָה פַאַרקֶערְט, אִיז דָאךְ וַויְיטֶער דּוּ, אוּן אַז דּוּ, אִיז דָאךְ דּוּ, דּוּ, דּוּ, דּוּ".

("You are found in the East, and also in the West. You are in the South and in the North. Above and below; You, You, You. When it is good, it is You; *chalilah* the opposite, is also You. And when it's You, it is You, it is You, You, You, You.")

During the singing, the Rebbe's heart overflows. His face is aflame, his eyes are closed, and his forehead is creased with concentration. The character of the Rebbe, the author of *Darchei Noam*, is one unit of emotion and logic, indissolubly connected. His physical form is down here, but his feelings and thoughts — so it seems — are far away in the expanses above.

בדרך ל'קידוש'

On the Way to Kiddush

There is no delicacy in the world that can compare with Yerushalmi *kugel*, made of thin noodles, round like a *shtreimel* and properly brown, giving off the steaming fragrance of pepper and caramel. It is said that every single noodle in a Yerushalmi *kugel* contains holy secrets. It's been prepared by Yerushalmi women for generations in honor of the Shabbos Queen, for a bar mitzvah or for an *aufruf* — when a *chosson* gets an *aliyah* before his wedding.

Authentic Yerushalmis know that *kugel* without a pickle is like a body without a soul — better if it didn't exist at all. On Erev Shabbos, the *gabbai* opens the can of pickles and cuts each pickle down its length into four quarters, as a money-saving tactic. Some prefer pickles in vinegar, but they are "*batel b'shishim*" among those who prefer pickles in brine. These facts are all trivial and inconsequential; the important thing is to have in mind to eat the *kugel* in honor of the Shabbos Queen.

התוֹרָהלֶ'ה של הילדים

The Children's Torah'le

The afternoon of Hoshana Rabbah is the seam between Sukkos and Simchas Torah. Passersby on the main street of Meah Shearim wear white *kittels,* and those coming home late from a Hoshana Rabbah davening in the *shtieblach* are still holding their *lulavim.* Sukkos songs can be heard emanating from the sukkahs — songs that blend together with the instructions of the wives and mothers busy getting ready for Shemini Atzeres.

Here, on the slopes of Choni Hame'agel Street, is a small stand selling miniature Sifrei Torah. Its owner, a colorful person who is not from the Yishuv Hayashan, presents his wares at this end of the street. The pure-eyed child wearing a yarmulke fingers the Sephardi Sefer Torah longingly. In his young mind, he imagines himself at his bar mitzvah, reading from the Sefer Torah, just like Tatty.

Now tell me: do touching scenes like this play out in other places?

מצפה לישועה
When Is Mashiach Coming?

Every night, at three o' clock in the morning, the Batei Ungarin neighborhood was witness to a wondrous scene: the tzaddik Rav Bunim Yoel Taussig, Rebbe of Mattersdorf, left his house and walked to his *beis midrash* to learn Torah until sunrise. In darkness and in light, during years of health and during the ones he was on dialysis, until his very last day, he never relinquished his habit of rising at three o'clock in the morning.

When he saw me as a child, he'd ask me if perhaps I knew when the *goel tzedek* would arrive. It wasn't just me that he asked, but everyone he happened to meet on his way. "I daven to merit to kiss Mashiach's hand," he told those who greeted him, his face shining with unbounded anticipation of Mashiach's arrival.

When Sukkos spread its wings in 2007, the residents were notified that the revered figure of the Rebbe would no longer embrace the neighborhood. Never again would they see him walking towards his nightly *avodah*, nor would they hear him ask, "*Nu, ven kumt shoin Mashiach?*"

Pictured is the Rebbe, wearing a white Hoshana Rabbah *kittel*, on his way to learn Torah, walking past the *hachnasas orchim* sukkah of Reb Leizer Hershler, who hosted a ragtag group of people with nowhere else to eat. The Rebbe is supported by a young child looking towards him admiringly. He's probably being asked that same eternal question, the question that hasn't been answered yet.

"When Chanukah arrives, the *ba'al teshuvah* stands by his windowsill and lights the lamps in the silver menorah that his wife purchased for him. He then takes his guitar, an instrument that he learned to strum while still in his secular life but that he now dedicates to holiness, and uses it to sing songs and praise the One Who made miracles for our forefathers, *bayamim hahem, ba'zeman hazeh.*

("Where *Ba'alei Teshuvah* Stand," page 349)

Chapter Eleven
Chanukah

הנרות הללו קודש הם
These Lights Are Holy

Rav Yitzchak Nosson Kuperstock *zt"l* began preparing for Chanukah at the very beginning of MarCheshvan, and his soul soared to peaks of *kedushah* when it arrived.

He prepared the lamps for his menorah before darkness descended. He would light two menorahs: one outside at the entrance to his home, and the second on the windowsill facing out, fulfilling all the *shittos*. He invested great effort in finding and preparing the wicks, locating the most *mehudar* olive oil, cleaning the glass containers, and filling them with oil.

When it was time to light the lamps in honor of the miracle of the Chashmonaim, Rav Yitzchak Nosson and his wife stood by themselves at the entrance to their home. There was no public in attendance, no noise and no tumult, no *gabbaim* or *meshamshim*. He fervently recited the *berachos*, his eyes shining from the tears generated by his devotion.

As he recited the *berachos*, his wife stood next to him with saintly fulfillment and pleasure in her eyes, and a pile of notes in her hands. Anyone in need of a *yeshuah* wrote his name and request on a small piece of paper, and the Rebbetzin read these during the *hadlakah* ceremony, an *eis ratzon*.

As the sun dimmed and darkness covered the earth, Rav Yitzchak Nosson stood before the pure flames, tears forming in his eyes. In a pleasant, stirring voice, he sang:

חֲשׂוֹף זְרוֹעַ קָדְשֶׁךָ, וְקָרֵב קֵץ הַיְשׁוּעָה.
נְקֹם נִקְמַת דַּם עֲבָדֶיךָ, מֵאֻמָּה הָרְשָׁעָה.
כִּי אָרְכָה לָנוּ הַיְשׁוּעָה, וְאֵין קֵץ לִימֵי הָרָעָה.
דְּחֵה אַדְמוֹן בְּצֵל צַלְמוֹן, הָקֵם לָנוּ רוֹעִים שִׁבְעָה.

נר מצווה ותורה אור
Mitzvos and Torah

From the dawn of his youth until the end of his days, Rav Avraham Yaakov Zeleznik's life was incessant Torah. When he was young he learned, and when he was an older man he taught with all the energy and joy of a young man.

From a young age, Rav Avraham Yaakov was educated in Etz Chaim, the first Torah institution outside of the walled city of Yerushalayim; when he was older he became its Rosh Yeshivah. Torah and humility were forever by his side; as we noted previously, the more the people of Yerushalayim grow in Torah, the more their stature is diminished in their own eyes.

Rav Avraham Yaakov lived in a small home in the Kerem neighborhood, where he devotedly served his Creator without cutting any corners and without shortcuts. He scrupulously followed the instructions of the *Shulchan Aruch*, without searching for leniencies. As Shabbos approached, he went out to greet it with his old *shtreimel* on his head, and when Shabbos left, he immediately washed his hands for *Melaveh Malkah*. A great, many-years-long story of *avodah* and *yirah* was folded up within his *shtreimel*, and the older it got the more glorious it became.

When Chanukah arrived, Rav Avraham Yaakov hurried to light the lamps in his simple menorah — small glasses for olive oil within a small aluminum box called a "*pushke*." When the sun disappeared below the horizon, he'd go to the *pushke* and recite the *berachah* with the restrained Yerushalmi devotion that doesn't incorporate shuckling or a blazing face: it's comprised simply of the purity of heart unique to Yerushalmi *talmidei chachamim*.

He sang "*Maoz Tzur*" to himself, using the popular melody that Yerushalmis personalized with their own nuances. If it was Motza'ei Shabbos, he'd light the *Melaveh Malkah* candles right after those of Chanukah, to fulfill the *pasuk*: *Yelchu mechayil el chayil, yeira'eh el Elokim b'Tzion*.

נר, שמן ונשמה
Lamp, Oil, and Soul

The tzaddik Rav Nachman Dubinki sat at the entrance of Batei Neitin reading *Sefer Tehillim* without interruption. He was a great *talmid chacham*; the cabinets in his home were full of manuscripts that he filled with his *chiddushei Torah*, but the many misfortunes brought to his home inspired him to fill most of his day with *Tehillim*.

He sat on a rickety bed supported by metal cans as he read *Tehillim* with a refined, pure face. When a photographer once told him, "Rabbeinu, I earn my living from photography; I would like to take a picture of the Rav learning," Rav Nachman answered, "Me, my only business is reading *Tehillim*."

On Chanukah, he donned his hat at twilight and lit in his window. The passersby watched admiringly as the illumination spread across his face — and it wasn't just the temporary illumination of the menorah's glow.

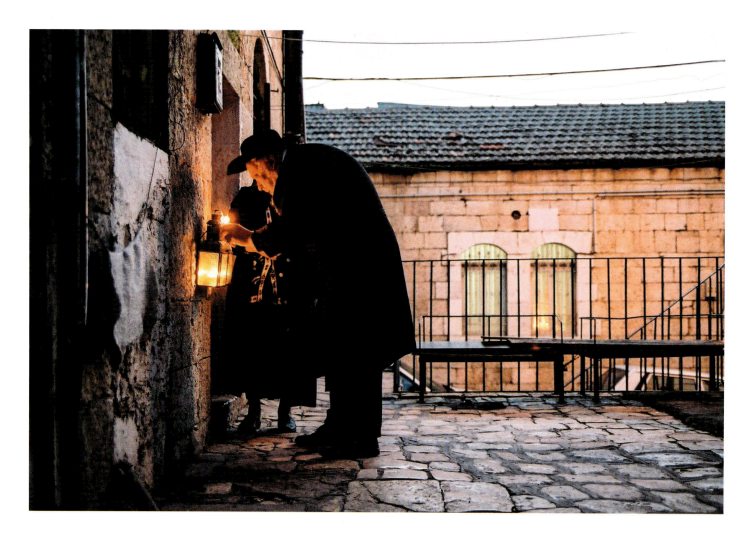

נר לאחד, נר למאה

For One, For All

The mitzvah of lighting lamps is cherished by the people of Yerushalayim. This is particularly true regarding the *perushim*, who meticulously light their Chanukah lamps after the sun sets.

Pictured is Rav Moshe Fisher, Rav of the Knesses Yisrael neighborhood and brother of Rav Yisrael Yaakov *zt"l*. He gives a Daf Yomi *shiur* in the neighborhood shul every single day.

Rav Moshe is modest and abstemious, like all wise Yerushalmis. A few floor *shmattas* hang to dry at the entrance to his home, as you can see in this picture, taken from above the ancient stone floor as Rav Moshe lights the flames in his *pushke*.

במקום שבעלי תשובה עומדים
Where Ba'alei Teshuvah Stand

One Shabbos during the 1980s, a red car got stuck in the Beis Yisrael neighborhood of Yerushalayim.

The *kanaim*, who saw that the red car was driven by a Jew on Shabbos, were incensed with holy passion and started screaming, "Shabbos... Shabbos!" and blocking the car. The Jew, who was ignorant of Torah and halachah, sat there confused and helpless.

A distinguished Karliner Chassid at the scene realized that the bewildered youth wasn't purposely desecrating Shabbos, but was just a *tinok shenishbah*. He went over to the youth trapped in the car and asked him to follow him. The youth's face lit up when he realized that an angel had arrived to rescue him: he abandoned his car and followed the Chassid.

When the two arrived at his home, the elderly Chassid handed his guest a yarmulke, made Kiddush, started to feed him, and spoke about the virtues and sanctity of Shabbos. When Shabbos was over, the youth returned to his car, but he never returned to his secularity. He drew close to Torah and was *chozer b'teshuvah*.

When this *ba'al teshuvah* married a *ba'alas teshuvah* like himself, the two decided to live in the old, picturesque Batei Broide neighborhood, where they would raise their next generation between the alleys of *kedushah*.

When Chanukah arrives, the *ba'al teshuvah* stands by his windowsill and lights the lamps in the silver menorah that his wife purchased for him. He then takes his guitar, an instrument that he learned to strum while still in his secular life but that he now dedicates to holiness, and uses it to sing songs and praise the One Who made miracles for our forefathers, *bayamim hahem, ba'zeman hazeh*.

Hundreds of secular tourists stand outside his window watching his holy *avodah*, until the hope flashes and sparks that perhaps they, too, will follow him in the light of Torah.

This *ba'al teshuvah* is an unusual sight in the scenery of Batei Broide, but he merited the respect of the neighborhood and its elders. He makes sure to pass on the same opportunity he received as a youth: every single Shabbos, he invites secular people to his home so that they can taste the light of the Shabbos Queen.

ומאירים את העולם
Lighting Up the World

For the children of Yerushalayim, Chanukah is the height of their aspirations. They daven constantly that Chanukah should arrive already, that their mothers should prepare latkes for them, and that they should be able to light the Chanukah menorah with pure olive oil, just like their fathers, and not with the colored candles used by little tots. Yerushalmi children scorn those colored paraffin candles — they're fine for toddlers and simple people, but not for the children of Yerushalayim who are *mesula'im b'paz* — worth their weight in gold.

Parts of this scene can't be expressed in the picture; the smell of frying latkes, the sound of oil popping in the pan, and the mother standing in the kitchen, one eye on the frying pan and the other watching her children standing next to their father, as the flame of the generations is lovingly transmitted to them.

האור כי טוב
Light Is Good

Rav Yosef ben Avraham Solich came from Latin America to settle among the *ovdei Hashem* in Batei Ungarin. The residents of the neighborhood adopted him as their son, married him off to a Jewish girl, and took care of all his needs until he was able to take care of himself.

On Chanukah, Rav Yosef Solich goes out with his innocent children, and patiently and serenely recites the *berachos*. In a Spanish-accented Yiddish, he tells his children about the miracles that were done to our forefathers. He, too, was included in these miracles because, as Chazal say, the *neshamos* of all *gerei tzedek* stood with Am Yisrael at Matan Torah.

"
On the fifteenth of Shevat, Rosh Hashanah of the trees, Rav Aharon Yosef invites the *talmidim* from neighboring yeshivos with unshaven beards to join him around his table. He serves his guests a collection of fruits *shenishtabcha bahem Eretz Yisrael* and then shares cryptic words of Kabbalah. For a short period of time, the beard-growing *bachurim* feel as though they've been taken to a different world — a hidden, lofty world, a world that is slowly disappearing.

("Sweet Fruits," page 357)

CHAPTER TWELVE
Tu Bi'Shevat

פירותיהם מתוקים

Sweet Fruits

One hundred measures of simplicity descended on the home of Rav Aharon Yosef Brizel in Batei Warsaw; no eye can ever get enough of the picturesqueness of his home and the simplicity of the manner of the person living within it. The archaic tiles on his floor speak of generations of old, his chairs are purple and, in the living room, his bed is squeaky and rickety — a type that can only be found in Batei Warsaw.

On the fifteenth of Shevat, Rosh Hashanah of the trees, Rav Aharon Yosef invites the *talmidim* from neighboring yeshivos with unshaven beards to join him around his table. He serves his guests a collection of fruits *shenishtabchah bahem Eretz Yisrael* and then shares cryptic words of Kabbalah. For a short period of time, the beard-growing *bachurim* feel as though they've been taken to a different world — a hidden, lofty world, a world that is slowly disappearing.

תפוחין קדישין

Holy Apples

The Zhvill Chassidus was led by holy tzaddikim: the patriarch, Rebbe Shlomke, a wonderworker who immigrated from Russia and then lived in Yerushalayim anonymously; Reb Shlomke's son, Rav Gedalyah Moshe, who led the Chassidus for just a few years but was still known as a wonderworker, and was buried in Sheikh Bader where his *kever* is a pilgrimage site; and Rebbe Mordche'le of Zhvill, who was also one of the exalted tzaddikim of Yerushalayim.

Rebbe Mordche'le was succeeded by his son, Rebbe Avraham, who led the Zhvill Chassidim in the same simple way as his fathers — without royal embellishments, without carved chairs, and without sixty "*giborim*" surrounding him. He was a humble tzaddik. He sat in simplicity before the bookcase that housed *sefarim* catalogued with a strip of orange tape. His house behind the *beis midrash* was modestly furnished but held countless *sefarim,* a testament to his avid love of learning.

During times of holiness, Rav Avraham of Zhvill adopted the role of his forefathers and led a *tisch* with sanctity and humility. At the height of the *tisch*, the Chassidim sang *teshuvah*-inspiring melodies that the dynasty's patriarch, Rebbe Micheli of Zlotschev, learned from his Rebbe, the Baal Shem Tov. On the fifteenth of Shevat, he'd toss apples to his Chassidim, a *minhag* that is a *segulah* for *yeshuos*. In other Chassidish courts apples are tossed on Motza'ei Simchas Torah, but Zhvill doesn't feel intimidated by what happens in other places. They follow their own unique customs transmitted to them by the tzaddikim of the dynasty.

In other Chassidish courts, whoever catches an apple is assured he'll find a *shidduch* that year. This photo depicts men who seem to be married — perhaps who have even married off their own kids — because in Zhvill, catching an apple thrown by the sacred hands of the Rebbe is a solid *segulah* for *yeshuos* in every area.

אילן, אילן
Fruits of the Tree

The Tu bi'Shevat Seder in Yerushalayim is far from the designer fruit baskets and eye-popping platters displayed in the magazines that have recently become so popular in *chareidi* areas. In Yerushalmi homes, fruits of the *shivas ha'minim* are preferred along with some almonds, peanuts, apples, and pears. "*Leder,*" or "fruit leather" (a thin strip of processed apricot, often used as the perfect prize for a Yerushalmi child who excels) is also served.

The Yurowitz Family is a distinguished family of Toldos Aharon. The head of the family, the tzaddik Rav Avraham, was a well-known *talmid chacham*. His *perishus* attracted a group of *bnei aliyah* who asked him to be their *rosh chaburah*. That was the start of the Vitebsk Kehillah on Avodas Yisrael Street that Rav Avraham ran as a sub-community to the Toldos Aharon Chassidus.

Rav Avraham's sons try to fill his place, following his death at a young age. One scion is this noble *avreich,* who lights the Tu bi'Shevat candles (as is customary in Yerushalayim) with his family, lofty *avreichim* like himself, watching him with devotion.

The children love Tu bi'Shevat. In the evening, they receive dried fruit — papaya, pineapple, and apricots — and in the morning, they're each given a *pekele* at the Tu bi'Shevat party in *cheder*.

"
A pair of cute twins came to their *melamed*'s house one Erev Purim. The *melamed* told them, "*Kinderlach*, dress up like two *avreichim* with a *shtreimel* and caftan." He then told a third child that he would read the *Megillah* — no small feat, because in Toldos Aharon, the Rebbe is the one who *leins* the *Megillah*! This child was playing the role of the holy Rebbe!

("Purim Rebbe," page 375)

Chapter Thirteen
Purim

מרבים בשמחה

Increasing the Joy

In Yerushalayim, they disagree with the prevalent assumption that costumes are for children. They believe the opposite is true: even adults, those with black hair and those with age-bleached hair, are commanded to be happy, and happiness means wearing a funny hat on one's head. This is an essential component of the character of the people of the Yishuv — they don't care what anybody else thinks.

If you happen to be walking on the streets of Meah Shearim on the day of *mikra Megillah*, you might notice a distinguished-looking person — someone who is a Mashgiach *kashrus* for the Badatz of the Ashkenazic community when it isn't Purim — dancing in the streets together with a grandson of Yossele Sheinberger zt"l from Toldos Aharon. One wears a white *shtreimel* while the other wears a *shtreimel* of some foreign, synthetic material.

These two share the streets with adorable children wearing masks on their faces — *"nezer"* (fake noses) and glasses called *"brillen"* — all in order to increase *simchah* and memorialize the miracle that happened to our forefathers, when the wicked Haman tried to stand up against us and ended up hanging from a tree.

הזקיף הקטן
THE YOUNG GUARD

Light years of cultural distance separate Buckingham Palace and the Pinsk-Karlin building in the old Beis Yisrael neighborhood, but even so, Yerushalmis familiar with the saying of Chazal, *Malchus ha'aretz domeh l'malchus Shamayim*, dress their children in the costume of the Queen's Guards, telling them, "My *tzaddikel*, you're a soldier of the King of the World."

The year this picture was taken was one of mourning in Yerushalayim. During this year, the Yishuv Hayashan lost Rav Levi Rabinowitz *zt"l*, one of its brilliant *talmidei chachamim*, and Rav Avraham Atick *zt"l*, a leading Rosh Yeshivah. This double loss was keenly felt and a sense of bereavement permeated the streets.

When Purim arrived, the Yishuv Hayashan displayed its strength with a unique blend of complete *simchah* and deep despondency. This boy is walking past the mourning notices for the *Gedolei Yisrael* that his mother davens for him to emulate. With a light heart, he carries a *mishloach manos* basket that his mother prepared for his rebbe in cheder.

The boy isn't aware that this cellophane package hides an envelope holding a 50- or 100-shekel bill — a gift from his parents for the one who teaches their son Torah.

בשמחה תמיד
Always Happy

For Yerushalmi children, Purim is full of pureness and joy, and quite different from Purim in other places. Firecrackers and other noisy nuisances are hardly heard.

The costumes of Yerushalmi children are unlike the costumes of other children. First of all, the costumes are chosen carefully, to be certain that they're uncontaminated by anything inappropriately secular.

Instead of prime ministers, there are successors of Aharon Hakohen; in place of famous professors, there are little Mordechais; instead of popular singers, Dovid Hamelech; and instead of long-haired gypsies, you'll see small Admors with woolen beards flowing down to their waists.

These costumes aren't manufactured by laborers in far-off China. They're the homemade creations of the loving mothers who sew the *"me'il"* with bells for Aharon Hakohen, garments of *"t'cheles and chur"* for Mordechai Hayehudi, and a robe for Dovid Hamelech.

This is Purim in the Toldos Aharon *cheder*.

At center, you can see Reb Simcha'le Breuer living up to his name — being happy and making other people happy. Around his neck hangs a display of three handmade dolls, the middle one stretching out his arm to accept tzedakah for the poor.

אדמו"ר ליום אחד

Purim Rebbe

A pair of cute twins came to their *melamed*'s house one Erev Purim. The *melamed* told them, "*Kinderlach*, dress up like two *avreichim* with a *shtreimel* and caftan." He then told a third child that he would read the *Megillah* — no small feat, because in Toldos Aharon, the Rebbe is the one who *leins* the *Megillah*! This child was playing the role of the holy Rebbe!

The Admor-for-a-day soon appeared with a white beard and fringed tallis, and was quickly surrounded by the twins — looking like Bigsan and Seresh would have looked had they been *chozer b'teshuvah* and become Chassidim. The children behind these three actors were like the Chassidim in the *beis midrash* on Purim night.

Was the *Megillah* actually *leined* or was this hemming and mumbling per the understanding of young children? We don't know what it was, but in either case the picture testifies that the pure-hearted Yerushalmi children don't aspire to be anyone else when they grow up other than the Rebbe himself.

והעיר ירושלים צהלה

Cheerful Yerushalayim

The elders of Yerushalayim read the *Megillah* with pure hearts. They are meticulous with its words and scrupulous with its letters. They don't read it as something retroactive, a historic story that once happened in Persian Shushan, but as current events. When Mordechai prays, they pray with him; when Esther pleads, they join her pleading; and when Haman realizes that there is no hope for him and falls at Esther's feet, they point a blaming finger at their persecutor and make sure that he doesn't evade the hangman's noose.

On the facing page is Rav Meir Grossman *zt"l*, an extraordinary man of *chesed*, someone who did much more *chesed* than the people crowned as men of *chesed* by local circulars and magazines. Here he sits in the Batei Ungarin Shul, aided by a magnifying glass, hewing mountains of satisfaction from the *mehudar Megillah* he had purchased with a big portion of his little money.

בקול, בכוח ובכוונה

Loud and Strong, with Meaning

Heichal Rabbi Yochanan of Chassidei Karlin Stolin is renowned as a place of fervent *tefillah*, where strident voices reach the heavens and spread out over the entire area. The Chassidim of Karlin daven powerfully, with shuckling and raised voices that inspire *kavanah*.

This is true throughout the entire year, but even more so on Purim. The joy of Purim in Karlin encompasses all ranks, ages, and status: young with old, *bnei Torah* and *ba'alei battim*. All celebrate together with gladness. When the name of the evil Haman is heard, the children wipe out Amalek with noisemak-

ers, caps, and other types of non-dangerous explosives, without any short-tempered or impatient people quieting them down. It's Purim, a time of joy for the children, and the exasperation of complaining adults is unbefitting today. This permissiveness is unique to Karlin; happy and lucky are its children. It is said in Karlin that *"Macho timcheh — nor mit simchah"* (Wipe out Amalek's name — only with joy).

Look at this child sitting on the stairs of the *beis midrash*, making noise with his gragger underneath the bottom of a Yerushalmi caftan that's folded with a coarse hem, like the many other people of Yerushalayim who inherit clothes from their grandfathers. As we've already mentioned, in the Yishuv Hayashan, what matters most is what's inside the heart; nobody pays attention to things such as fashion, which changes from day to day and dissipates as quickly as a Purim firecracker.

Above is the tzaddik Rav Luzer Brizel *zt"l*, a Yerushalmi *mekubal* who concentrates on the *Megillah* and sculpts holy, kabbalistic secrets from its letters.

לימוד של פורים

Purim Torah

It's amusing to wander through Meah Shearim Street on Purim and see people with battered *shtreimel*s passed down from the Baal Shem Tov and his disciples. There is no way of knowing if the ancient-*shtreimel* wearer is so poor that he has no choice but to wear fox-tails inherited from his father's fathers in the generation of Rav Shmuel Salant, or if he has a magnificent, new *shtreimel* at home, but chose to take out this antique from storage as a joke, to symbolize his joyfulness.

There are no clear signs to identify what you're seeing, but we do have one tip: Don't focus on the exterior garments. Instead,

concentrate on the wonderful customs that have settled in Yerushalayim and other *chareidi* strongholds. At the height of this day, fathers and sons detach themselves from *mishlochei manos*, cellophane, and *hamantashen* and gather together at a local *beis midrash* to learn Torah.

Mah nehedar, how wondrous is the sight of cherub-faced youth sitting next to the elders of the nation. One boy learns with his grandfather "Zeide Krauss." He's dressed up like a Yemenite who just recently left Sa'ana, and only the color of his skin testifies that he's a fiftieth generation Ashkenazi Yerushalmi. Another boy learns with his father dressed up like a tall-*spudik*ed Admor with thousands of Chassidim at his *tisch*. *Mishlochei manos* are being sent all around, Purim noises fill the air around them — but they need nothing other than the four *amos* of Torah study.

פורים דמתמידים

Purim of Masmidim

Purim in the Masmidim community is a byword. It's the day on which the community members get together, the old with the young. They all wear the same uniform: a golden "zebra" — worn also by the unmarried boys on Purim — and a red turban with a tassel at its top and a star at its front.

This turban that they call a *"feskeh"* is unique to the Masmidim community. Other communities, some of which separated from the Masmidim, adopted turbans of other colors and shapes. Each community is identified by its particular style, which demonstrates that Yerushalmi *kehillos* are careful to preserve their distinctiveness even on Purim.

But why get stuck on minor external details? The primary point is the internal *simchah*, and the *simchas Purim* in Masmidim can overpower even the harshest, coarsest of hearts.

On Purim, the Rosh Kehillah, Rav Leib Mintzberg *zt"l*, wore a Rebbishe *"kolfik"* and sat surrounded by the distinguished members of the *kehillah* — Rav Meir Sirota, Rav Yosef Hirschman, and Rav Ben Zion Gutfarb. The latter wore a Moroccan jalabiya, like a "Baba" born in Marrakesh. In honor of this Purim costume, the members of Masmidim allow themselves to call him Baba Tzion. A *frelichen* Purim!

השמח בחלקו

Happy with His Portion

Rav Uri Weinberg zt"l had nothing, yet he had everything.

He was childless and alone. Born in Germany, his very essence was meticulous *yekkishness*. On Wednesdays, he'd take his baskets to the *shuk* to buy live fish and meat from the butcher, which he prepared on kerosene burners.

Rav Uri woke up early to daven *vasikin* in the Batei Neitin Shul. Later, for Minchah and Maariv, he'd walk over to the Mir Yeshivah, where he invited American *bachurim* to eat in his dark apartment on Friday nights. His apartment had no electric lighting, only kerosene lamps that made shadows on the ceiling, which terrified me as a child.

Though he was alone in the world, the power of his *simchas hachaim* infected everyone he met. The glee of a million dollar-lottery winner couldn't compare to the joy of Rav Uri when he lit the Chanukah menorah in the tin box fashioned by his own hands, when he built his sukkah from moldy, one hundred-year-old palm leaves, or when he listened to the *Megillah* reading from the ancient *klaf Megillah* that he owned.

Here he is, standing in the Batei Neitin Shul, listening with *yekkish* meticulousness to the miracles of *Megillas Esther,* happy and satisfied with his lot. In the picture on the facing page, he stands next to the tzaddik Rav Nachman Dubinki zt"l, who listens with a pure heart to the wonders that were orchestrated for his forefathers in the times of Mordechai and Esther in Shushan HaBirah.

אַ זֵיידֵאלֵע מִיט אַ בָּאבִּיטְשְׁקֵע

A Zeidy with a Bubby

Whoever said, "The world belongs to the young," never visited Meah Shearim. If he had, he would rethink his dubious statement.

In Meah Shearim they maintain that *"Di velt gehrt tzu di alte* — The world belongs to the old." They, the ones old in numbers, are the ones worthy of grandeur. They, the ones who acquired wisdom and experienced numerous adventures, are worthy of admiration. Because this is fact, the elders of the community, its old men and women, remnants and vestiges of the *dor de'ah*, are honored and respected.

It is said that a person's Purim costume expresses his aspirations and, if so, the children of Meah Shearim aspire to be old men and women.

They love the costume *"a Zeidaleh mit a Babitshke"* — a grandfather with a grandmother. The advantage of this costume is that it doesn't involve a lot of work or expense. All it takes is a shabby *kapalush* (hat), a threadbare caftan, a discarded *tichele,* and an old shawl — all of which are easily accessible. The costume is also absolutely enchanting. Take a look at the picture and see for yourself.

פורים אצל רבי וֶועלְוְול
Purim by Rav Velvel

Over Purim, the dining room of the tzaddik Rav Velvel Eisenbach zt"l, a Yerushalmi *oved Hashem* and patriarch of one of the city's largest families, hosts hundreds of grandchildren who come and go in shifts. If his descendants would join together for the Purim *seudah*, they would need a table the size of the entire Batei Ungarin neighborhood!

The first group of great-grandchildren bring *mishloach manos* that includes sugar, banana liquor, "Berman" cookies, and cans of pineapple in light syrup. Rav Velvel, abstemious and ascetic, doesn't taste any of it; instead, he sits and teaches *ahavas haTorah* and *yiras Shamayim* to his descendants.

Rav Velvel was a *"shatkan"* — he spoke sparingly. But one day a year, on Purim, he deviated from his usual characteristics and told his grandchildren a little about himself, until the grandchildren fought with one another so they could hear their grandfather's fascinating history.

אחרית דבר

Afterword

Menachem Av, 2019

One of the unique characteristics of the Meah Shearim neighborhood is the perfect integration of the ancient appearance of its homes and alleys and the ancient appearance of its residents.

In the twenty years during which I wandered around Meah Shearim, I noticed that there is another close connection between the people and their environment: it seems that when an elderly person is uprooted from the scenery of Meah Shearim and moved to Har HaZeisim, the walls of his house are uprooted along with him.

For example, just recently the magical neighborhood of Batei Wittenberg was fenced off in preparation for demolition and reconstruction. Just like we lost the presence of Rav Elimelech Cheshin, the *melamed* and tzaddik who lived in that neighborhood, it seems that the authentic Batei Wittenberg neighborhood is also moving towards extinction.

I, personally, mourn this loss, the loss of both the elderly residents of the neighborhood who are moving to the Next World and the loss of every old, dilapidated building that is disappearing from this rare, beautiful place.

It's true that there is joy and significance in the rebuilding of Yerushalayim, but my heart tells me that this new construction, this modern, superficial style, is an expression of the *churban*.

I believe that my mourning is reminiscent in some way to the cries of the elderly when they saw the Second Beis HaMikdash, and wept as they compared it to the First.

I don't mourn the exterior expressions of Meah Shearim that are disappearing, but the deep, profound beauty that reflected the deep substance of the residents of the neighborhood who, unfortunately, are also disappearing.

Dor holech v'dor ba — One generation goes and another generation comes...

I'm sure that there are other angles of this neighborhood and the heartwarming appearance of its residents that I haven't yet succeeded in documenting. But I believe that this album provides a small peephole through which one can acquire a genuine and profound view of a pure world that is connected directly to the *Melech Ha'Olam*.

It's impossible for me to properly express the significance of the positive influences I received from this neighborhood. I merely tried to share a taste of this neighborhood through these pictures. I tried to give you a taste of this holy, refined, special flavor of the Meah Shearim neighborhood, whose fragrance is powerful enough to drift to distant lands and is treasured in the hearts of so many people.

Baruch Yaari